# BEAUTY
## in the BreakUp

**by** *Julie Tuton*

Penny,

keep choosing to be
the beauty of you.

♡ —
Julie

BEAUTY in the BreakUp
Copyright © 2017 Julie Tuton
ISBN: 978-1-63493-130-4

Published by
Access Consciousness Publishing, LLC
www.accessconsciousnesspublishing.com

Printed in the United States of America

Ease, Joy and Glory

# Table of Contents

## Step 2  **Dissolving Past Trauma**

## Step 3  **Navigation System**

## Step 4  **Breaking through Barriers**

## Step 5  **Conscious Creation**

## Step 6  **Maintenance System**

# Introduction

As early as I can remember I had a really big dream to inspire the world. I am not sure where it came from, and it doesn't matter. That dream was clearly my target in life. I never thought it would include writing a book, and especially never thought it would have anything to do with the subject of divorce. My parents divorced when I was nine, and I decided then that I would never do that to my kids.

Years later, in my early twenties, I created a jewelry and art business just for the fun of it. I loved creating beauty in the world, and these were a few areas that were easy and fun for me. Things really took off when one of my inspirational products was selected to be featured on the Oprah Winfrey show—a pretty big first step toward realizing that dream of inspiring the world.

People from all over the globe seemed to be drawn to and began ordering my handmade, pocket-sized affirmation stones I called MagicStones®. I sent stones to Europe, the Netherlands, Australia, Singapore, all over the US and Canada. The Smithsonian Institute ordered them; gift shops and boutiques that had been previous customers tripled their orders; famous people—including Hollywood stars and the President of the United States—received them as gifts. Hundreds of letters poured in telling me stories of how these people had become inspired to create magic and miracles in their lives because of my stones. It was amazing, magical, beyond what I had imagined... yet somehow it was not enough.

That dream to inspire the world kept me continually looking for greater possibilities.

Being so busy creating a successful business kept me from looking at the things that were not working so well for me in my personal life; specifically, in my marriage. At 39 I felt old, ugly, and undesirable. I was able to suppress those feelings for a long time... until I just couldn't anymore. I knew so much more was possible. Somewhere, somehow I knew that our marriage could have more joy, more nurturing, more receiving, and we could contribute so much more to each other. It was difficult to watch my husband and partner shrink back from creating his life and from being everything he could be. What would inspire him to be the greatness I saw in him that he would only let be an occasional glimmer? And where was I resisting being everything I could be? What were we teaching our children with the choices we were making?

I kept wondering what else was possible to inspire me, my family, and the world that I hadn't considered yet? Soon after, I found the tools of Access Consciousness® and my life—actually, all of our lives—haven't been the same since.

When I first learned these tools I applied them to every aspect of my life, including my marriage, hoping they might fix what had not been working. After five years of trying to fix my relationship, I realized that making a different choice (the choice to end my marriage) was actually lighter and more true to my deeper desires. Using the tools for our breakup created an incredible ease and space in the aspect I had previously feared was unchangeable. In order to get clear, I had to be willing to look deeply into the hidden places where I had swept away my true desires, and be willing to face the apprehension. I had to lower my barriers, be honest with myself and get a sense of which things were aware-ness, and which were judgments.

The reason this is important is that when we're in judgment of our partners, or ourselves for that matter, we're not seeing what truly is, we're seeing a construct of what we've decided was true based on a conclusion that justifies the rightness of our point of view. As this book unfolds, I will introduce you to some very pow-erful tools for separating judgment from awareness. One of the things that often holds people stagnant for so long is the worry, "What if I'm wrong? What if I get divorced and regret my deci-sion?" Trying to figure out what is the right or best choice, not wanting to make a wrong decision, keeps you in a holding pat-tern of judgment. Getting clear on which of your thoughts are judgments and which are your true awareness keeps this from becoming your reality.

Once it started to become apparent—again, by using the tools in this book—that it was truly my awareness, and not just fear or judgment that I was perceiving, it became so much lighter to take the first steps down the path toward separation. Choosing from awareness gave us such different possibilities! Literally everyone who knew us or crossed our path was amazed at how light and spacious the divorce process was for us. Even our mediator won-dered, "Are you sure you two want to get a divorce? You are so kind to each other." For me, I realized I had to "un-divorce" my-self, which happened to include divorce from my husband.

This book outlines the steps and tools I used myself and with my clients in my Consciously Uncoupling coaching program, orga-nized into a protocol for you to utilize. You can use these tools to create changes in your relationship so that it works better for you, or so you can have ease in your breakup.

Breaking up may not end up being your choice. By following these simple steps, some people find that their relationship becomes more loving and intimate. Part of this coaching program is getting out of judgment of yourself and your partner, which allows space for infinite possibilities to open up, from which you can make your most conscious choices.

**BEAUTY in the BreakUp** is not only about introducing pragmatic tools you can use to undo the places in your life where you are stuck, entangled, or lack clarity, it's also about demonstrating— with stories of true accounts of real people creating real beauty— to show you how to use those tools so you can move forward on whichever path you choose. I invite you to play with these tools in the 6 Steps I have outlined here in this book. See how you can create changes for yourself. You may choose greater awareness, and you may step into the beauty of truly being YOU.

Whatever status your relationship is currently, holding on and trying to force it to work is not going to make it better. Rather, when you are *willing* to completely let go of something is when you can have it fully. So if you were to transition into being willing to let go, start fresh, or create something new, how much more present would you be? How much more beauty would be possible in the future that you're creating?

# Where are You?

## Afraid of rocking the boat?

Contemplating a breakup or divorce is not something you talk about. It starts with a foreboding sense deep within, which bubbles up more and more the longer you avoid it. You know when you *know* that something is just not right? But you stuff it down because you don't want to upset things, which then makes you start to feel panic, stress, fear, and a number of other emotions that get you so tied up you can't even remember that you knew?!? What if avoiding what you know, avoiding the awareness, avoiding rocking the boat, actually makes the boat sink deeper, faster? Avoiding what you know is the beginning of what is called "divorcing you." In actuality, acknowledging that something needs to change begins to calm the waters.

This is where I was 15 years ago. I *knew* that deep down I wasn't happy. I *knew* that I had diverged so far off course that I could not take another step further or I might risk losing *myself* completely. I *knew* that something had to change in my life. Yet I didn't want to rock the boat. In everyone else's eyes, my life was a success. I had a lot to be grateful for. I had a handsome husband, two beautiful children, a growing business doing something I loved, we owned a house in my favorite city, San Francisco... everything that is the picture of success in this reality. How could I risk changing that? I could lose everything.

*Divorcing you is having the awareness of something, and refusing to acknowledge it. You divorce you to keep the relationship intact.*

Is there somewhere inside where you know that your relationship is not working for you and something has to change? Do you have this deep nagging feeling that doesn't seem to go away? Yes, it is possible to bury it for a while; ignore it; shove it out of your mind... but does it keeps coming back?

I had grown exhausted from trying to suppress everything. There really wasn't anyone I could turn to for advice. Even scouring the internet for something that would help me know what to do, turned up empty. Just when I thought I couldn't stand it anymore, I found and began using the tools of Access Consciousness. These tools were like a beacon, enlightening an easier way to navigate life, specifically the rocky terrain of contemplating separation and divorce. When I was confused, afraid, constricted, unsure, stressed or didn't feel like I had the strength to go through with it, I reached for these tools again and again, and they always created more space and ease. They were instrumental in my having this greater possibility. I'd like to share them with you in the hope that they may make it easier for you, too, to traverse whichever path you choose to take moving forward from here.

*What do you know, or are you pretending that you don't know, that if you would be honest with yourself, would allow your entire life to shift and change for the better?*

This question brings us to the first tool I'd like to offer you:

## Tool #1: Lower your barriers, and go into question: "What is true for me?"

Find a quiet space to sit down, relax, and get comfortable. Only when you're willing to be honest with yourself and look at what is true for you, can you begin to change things. Now, lower your barriers; push them down, and begin to look at the things you have been resisting—the things you've swept under the carpet, or put it in the way, way back of the closet but you know are still there. Ask yourself: "What is true for me? Is this relationship working for me?" Be willing to look rather than hiding what you know. By hiding and not wanting to look, you are putting up barriers to your own awareness. True vulnerability means not having any barriers to your awareness.

At this point, you may just think this is what relationship is... most other couples do not seem to be doing anything different. But somewhere you have an awareness that living with these difficulties isn't working for you. You may only be aware of the gnawing irritations that have been grating on you for years. Still, acknowledge them. Be willing to look at what is. And then ask a question.

Asking a question is like opening a door to the places you've made mysterious to yourself. You don't have to go wandering around looking for anything, or start gathering up your evidence of how your partner is wrong. That behavior perpetuates ugliness. Let's just set aside this right/wrong business—we have other tools for that! For now just allow the questions to BE. We have been taught to look for immediate answers or to come to conclusions. However I'm asking you to simply ask the questions and then let them percolate; allow the questions to go out into the universe and notice when responses show up. It may take moments, hours, days, or even weeks. As you become aware of the different possibilities that present themselves, you can then choose an action if necessary, or just receive the new awareness.

Continue asking questions: *What will be rewarding for me and everyone else concerned? What conscious choice can I make for a more enjoyable living?*

## What is a conscious choice?

Consciousness is the awareness of everything as it is, with no judgment. It is one of the most attractive qualities you can BE. What would it be like to make choices from total awareness of what those choices would create, rather than what we've been told is right or wrong, good or bad? How much more ease would that create in your world? For example, if you were willing to let go of the conclusion that breaking up has to be a bad thing, would that allow you to have even a little less judgment of yourself for considering it?

What if you didn't have to fight to create the change or separation you want? So many times you hear of horribly ugly, destructive breakups, where each person carries forward the baggage of everything they made wrong, significant, real and unchangeable about their partner. What if you didn't have to be wrong, or blame one another? What if you lowered your barriers and took an honest appraisal? If you could see your partner through a new lens, one that didn't filter him/her through your judgments, could you receive them in a different way? If the relationship isn't working anymore, could you choose to move on peacefully? There really is no story, no reason, no justification necessary. You don't have to carry that heavy load of negativity into your future. Did you know that you can just lay it all down? It is just a choice... a *conscious* choice.

Access tools and processes assist you in gaining and **following your awareness**. While expanding my awareness and learning how to choose *for* it, I couldn't choose *against* it or stuff it anymore. It was too painful. When I started to use the tools I'm introducing to you here, I began to realize how much of ME I had been cutting off to make my relationship work. I was divorcing myself to stay married.

Simply starting to lower my own barriers and look at little things began to open up more and more awareness of choices I made against my knowing and against what I truly desired. Along with honest appraisal of where I had separated from *me*, I simultaneously began to ask myself questions to get back in touch with those severed pieces: *If I were actually choosing for me here, what would I choose?* I began to be more of my true self. The more I changed, the more I realized, *You know what? This marriage doesn't really work for me! Our priorities are very different. It's not fun anymore. I wonder what else is possible? What beauty could we create if we were to breakup?*

As I transitioned from surreptitiously contemplating separation and inching forward with baby steps, to finally acknowledging that I was ready to end my marriage and asking questions to get in touch with the Me I had cut myself off from, I had to then look ahead to Step 2: how to dissolve the entanglements of the past and move forward in the kindest way possible. I didn't want to hurt anyone, and that included me... for the first time.

What if separating didn't have to come from the anger, the force, the hurt and upset associated with most breakups? What if it was simply a choice? A simple, *conscious* choice.

Sometimes relationships run their course. At first, I didn't want to acknowledge this for myself and wouldn't even look at it. All of my justifications would come up: *My parents divorced... I decided I would never get divorced... I hate that word, DIVORCE... I like being married... We have two young kids... I don't want to be a single mom... Divorce would be admitting failure.*

Notice there were no questions in that mess? There were judgments, decisions I had made as a kid, and conflicting points of view. It took me five years of using the Access tools to try to *fix* my relationship before I was willing to ask questions about leaving my marriage. (Hopefully this book can save you some of the time and effort I put in).

Fixing a relationship is often unsuccessful because of the judgments and conclusions in place. When you come from a specific point of view about what is wrong, you solidify things so they can't change. It's like trying to treat the symptoms, rather than resolving the root of the issue. Doing something different is key, like asking questions from a place of vulnerability, which opens up the possibility of change.

As I mentioned, I was afraid to look into the future. I thought I was fearful of change. It was uncomfortable to consider moving blindly into an unknown place. But eventually, I couldn't hold myself back anymore. I had gotten to the point where I just had to lower my barriers and take a look.

As I lowered my barriers and got vulnerable with myself, I used deep questions (and the awareness they generated) to expand my choice into the future to sense what those choices would create. Using this technique (Tool #9) assuaged the feelings of blindly jumping into the unknown, and helped me get a sense of what my life would be like based on what my choices would create. I will expand on how you can use this tool for yourself later in this book.

From a place of **true curiosity** I played with this tool, looking at different aspects. If I chose to leave the relationship, what would it be like for me, for my children, for my ex-husband-to-be, for the family? Each question brought an immediate awareness of expansion. And I knew from using Tool #6 that expansion/light-ness is a sign of something that is true for me and would expand my life/possibilities, and that following that feeling was a con-scious choice. Going against that awareness would feel contract-ed and be an anti-conscious choice.

But how was it possible that divorce could be a conscious choice? I believed other people's points of view that divorce was wrong, a bad thing, a failure, and lead to devastation for most... especially the children (although from my point of view I turned out ok; I could even see the blessing in my parents' choices). I pulled in all the courage I could muster and started asking even deeper questions. Each time I looked into the potential energy created by that possible future, it was much more expansive to move on than to stay married. Weird. Different than I had imagined. When something doesn't work for you, or your relationship doesn't work for you, that does not mean that it's a failure!

*Everywhere you've decided you're a failure because a relationship isn't working, or didn't work, or wherever you have tried to con-tract, force yourself to fit, or shut off your true desires to make it work, and it still doesn't work, and you're making yourself wrong for it, will you let that go and consider other possibilities, please?* Let's come out of the decided wrongness, and begin asking ques-tions to create new possibilities.

Asking questions allows you to start to perceive different possibilities that you will never know if you don't ask. That's the difficulty with deciding something—whatever you decide, you are right. And you are stuck. It is a conclusion. And what does conclusion mean? Ending! There is nothing else possible from your point of view. If something doesn't work, OK. Acknowledge you're stuck and ask a question like: "Will this relationship truly work for me?" "What would my life be like if we made a different choice?" "What if we separated or divorced?" "What would it be like for the kids?" "What would this choice create for my partner?"

Sometimes the "lighter" choice (the one that feels expansive) is to remain in the relationship, and sometimes it is lighter to break up. If it is clear that moving on is your *conscious* choice, you can start to go deeper into the "how": *How can we move forward in the kindest way possible?—a way that doesn't include anger and rancor?*

To go deeper, you must be vulnerable with yourself to honestly look at and observe what IS. *What works, and what doesn't work? What is required for this to work for me, and everyone involved?* You can create so much ease and space asking these questions. Moving forward could be (and should be) an expansive, beautiful adventure.

I'm not saying the transition will have no challenges—you will be challenged. You may even doubt yourself—many times. Although our divorce was smooth and easy, afterward we did hit some bumps and some huge rough patches. When difficulties came up, my favorite tool (Tool #3 of this book) was getting my Bars® run. Access Bars is a gentle energetic body process that can free you from the stuck feeling of "no choice." It cleared away all of the upset so that I could deal with the situation from a space of observation, rather than judgment.

It takes practice to trust yourself. Keep asking, keep choosing, and you will find things getting much better. Believe me, when you start making conscious choices, your entire life gets way better than you have ever thought possible—really!

If you are contemplating a breakup, are in the process of divorce, or have already gone through the motions and would like to move forward free from stress and trauma, I have created a 6 step program that allows you to unwind, dissolve the past, learn a system of navigation to gain clarity on what you truly desire, and start creating the future you'd love to be living. In the pages that follow are some of the tools I used both on myself and with my clients for consciously uncoupling and finding **BEAUTY in the BreakUp.**

- Step 1 - Unwinding
- Step 2 - Dissolving Past Trauma
- Step 3 - Navigation System
- Step 4 - Breaking through Barriers
- Step 5 - Conscious Creation
- Step 6 - Maintenance System

Thank you for having the courage to explore some of the places you may not have wanted to go before. Breaking up might seem kind of scary, but I have found that what we think is fear, actually can be excitement. Let's move through this together. Any area of your life that is not working the way you'd like it to is a place that we can change. Letting go gives you the unique perspective of creating something new, beautiful and different. Your true desires emerge when you give yourself permission to choose.

Just reading about these steps and having the tools will not create the change. *You'll need to use them.* Use them in your unique way. Just as an artist with a set of paints and brushes can paint a different picture every day, so can you paint your amazing, juicy, inspired life in exactly the way you desire. The canvas is waiting. Make your mark. What beauty can you create in *your* breakup?

"If you didn't do divorce from the anger it took
to create separation but from the possibility of
what separation could create, what really could
be created that we haven't even considered?"

—Gary Douglas, Founder *Access Consciousness*

# Step 1

## Unwinding

### Creating space to reclaim YOU by untangling from the relationship

*Journal entry—written in 2009.*

*We began the process of the paperwork for a dissolution of marriage agreement today. I realize just how much I made the relationship my entire life. We had woven ourselves together in just about every aspect. We lived together, worked together, ate together, traveled together... we were hardly apart. There were no places where one existed without the other. We would always opt to be together, rather than choose to do something with a friend or on our own. I rationalized that we just liked being together, that we were best friends.*

*Now it feels like I'm losing my life. It is a strange feeling. Mixed feelings—freedom, loss, excitement, anxiety, fear of the unknown. And yet, looking back, there is no way I'd turn around. Maybe I'm actually feeling excitement? What would I truly like as my life now? Moving onward in the journey; Creating new adventures; Being excited about what is next. That is the possibility I'd like for myself and my family.*

Whatever the reason for your possible breakup, whether you simply have drifted apart, grown distant, or are unable to rekindle or recreate what your relationship used to be, your first step will be untangling from your investment in your idea of the relationship. To some, the relationship is like a distant memory, a faded photo, no longer present to touch. Some of you might be the ones "being left." You might feel like it came as a shock or surprise. And some of you will untangle from the notion of Two becoming One.

To start unwinding the entanglement you have created as your relationship, you must have space and relaxation to reclaim you. I'm going to ask you some tough questions. Will you lower your barriers and take a deep honest look inside?

*Were you truly happy? Was your partner truly happy? Were there things you hid from yourself to make the relationship work? Did you lose yourself in the process?*

If you are anything like we were, you may have woven yourselves so tightly into *Couple* that you don't exist as *You* anymore. I hardly noticed how much this was true for me, until one day I needed to fly home for a funeral and left the kids home with Dad. As I walked through the security gates alone, it was as if I was walking out of this reality into my true reality, which had been placed on hold so many years before. It was strange and familiar all at the same time. I felt younger, freer, and more *me*. I realized I had just begun to relax and have some space.

With relaxation and space, that tightness can start to unwind itself, freeing you from decisions and judgments that keep you from knowing that *anything else is possible.* In this space you are able to unwind that tangle, and recall who you are.

Finding nurturing ways to relax and have space for yourself is key for living a happy life. As well, relaxation and space are especially important during a time of transition like breakups, separation and divorce. I've always found that being in nature invites me into deep relaxation. The earth has such a tender, healing energy. If you can get outdoors, you might try walking in the woods, or going for a swim in the ocean. Also treating yourself to a massage, or being around children can be nice. Coming out of judgment of yourself, stepping into the space of awareness and allowance can take that heavy burden of other people's priorities off your shoulders.

Another way to find that deep peace of relaxation and space is listening to my special audio "Unwinding," which can help ease your worried mind. It is sort of like a guided meditation, combined with clearings and energies that invite you to relax and let go. Some clients like to listen as they fall asleep to have a deeper, more peaceful rest.

I will introduce other tools to create space in more detail as the pages unfold. Find ways to relax that work for you. Give yourself this gift during the process of a breakup... and maybe continue to do so afterward, just because it works for you!

Taking an hour a day, and a day a week, to nurture your body and soul will change your life!

—Gary Douglas

## How Decisions limit you—how you got tangled up in your current relationship

As a young girl I had a dad that wasn't home very much. He worked long hours. My mom did her best to raise us. We had fun outdoor activities, several pets including fish, bunnies, a pony and a cat, plus a large vegetable garden. I remember my mom used to jokingly tell her friends that she asked us kids one day, "Who haven't you seen in a few days?" We all said in unison, "Daddy?!" But she said, "No... Blacky!" (the cat who got sick and had to be put to sleep).

Not long after this we moved to a different state, as my dad got promoted to a new division of his company. We moved into a large house in a nice neighborhood. Even though it looked pretty on the outside, it was filled with unhappiness. My brother and I would wake up in the middle of the night and sneak downstairs to get a snack when we'd turn the corner towards the kitchen and hear my parents fighting. We'd hug each other for comfort and run back to bed. Within the year my parents got divorced. My dad moved far away and we saw him even less... about once a year, sometimes every other year. I was nine years old.

What decisions did I make then? I remember deciding that I would *never, ever, ever, ever* make that same choice. I was going to be *absolutely sure* that I would *marry the right man*, and **never, ever, ever get divorced.** I wouldn't do that to my kids. And I would spend a lot of time WITH my husband. Guess what stuck me for 20+ years of marriage? Those decisions.

How did that affect all my future relationships? Looking at it now, I realize how much those decisions have affected my entire life. With each and every relationship I ever had, we spent all of our time together! There was no personal space, time for friends on my own, or alone time—the exact opposite of what my parents had created.

Taking irrational points of view from childhood and making solid decisions based on them had not made my life any better than my parents'. If anything, it bound me to a hidden agenda. I hadn't even realized I was still functioning from my childish ideas. I know now that having my awareness of how much space I require, what is fun for me, and being willing to follow the energy of lightness and expansive possibilities is what actually creates a happier, more fulfilling life for me.

Perhaps you've had the opposite experience, each of you continually breaking away to do things on your own, until you realize that the connection you once had is gone. There is no energy there. You may have tried to rekindle the sparks that brought you together in the first place. But if nothing is working, have you considered that the relationship might be completed? If this doesn't match your dreams of happily ever after, you will keep trying to resuscitate it unsuccessfully.

Can you now see how decisions, or agendas, can create future problems? And can you see that when you forget you ever made them, that it might be difficult to get to the root of the problem and make changes? The cool thing is that I have found a way to clear these decisions and agendas that we have hidden from ourselves, and in doing so, allow for different possibilities for life and living.

It is actually really easy, and you don't have to go into the emotional trauma and drama of your childhood to clear it out. This is due to the nature of the Access tools... **they work with the**

**energy.** All of the places you are stuck, have a fixed point of view, or decision/judgment/belief or a truth and a lie tied together, can be accessed energetically; we can clear those blocks without cognitively digging through the garbage can of your past.

*Think it's not possible? Then you're right... you can't change a thing with that point of view. Because your point of view creates what shows up in your life.*

Are you curious about changing your points of view? Now we have some possibilities to explore...

What if every decision, ideal dream, and fantasy about the way you've decided your life is *supposed* to be, keeps you tightly wound around and bound to the rigid, fixed idea of what you *think* you want? If you were to unwind, relax, back off trying to figure everything out, and ask some questions, I wonder what other possibilities might start showing up?

Everywhere you have been trying to get it *right*, and get what you *think* you want, requires that you **judge** where you are at every moment. Judgment contracts your being, your body, and blocks any other possibility from showing up. What if there is no right or wrong? How much more energy would you have if you weren't holding all those judgments in place? It takes a huge amount of energy to contract the infinite being you are in order to cut off the expansive space, capacities and possibilities that are your true nature.

*What have you decided is not possible, that if you were willing to drop that point of view, would allow things to shift and the universe deliver to you everything you desire but haven't yet asked for? Let's take a deep breath here and let it all go.*

So what are some more ways to unwind? This brings us to our second tool for navigating the landscape of breakups: Interesting Point of View.

## Tool #2: To begin to get free of your own decisions and conclusions, start seeing everything as an Interesting Point of View (IPOV)

When you take a fixed point of view you can't see any other possibilities, you just start to gather evidence to justify your having the point of view in the first place. That even feels kind of heavy as I type it out. Can you sense that too? The way to become free is to have the ability to see all points of view, not just the one you defend. This is also what is called being in "allowance." **Being in allowance** gives you freedom from your points of view, as well as other people's points of view. So in using this tool, you are clearing your fixed points of view to create more space and allowance for you and everyone else.

How do you use this tool? When you are aware of something that triggers you, makes you feel stuck with no choice, or you are looping back into some issue that you can't seem to let go of, just take a breath and say to yourself: "Interesting point of view I have this point of view." Take another breath. Allow a little space to open up. Then repeat it again 2-10 times, or until the energetic charge you felt dissipates.

Let's *clear* some points of view right now. Take one aspect that bothers you about your relationship as it is currently. Choose something that irritates you about your partner, like a silly hab-it or mannerism (perhaps one that used to be endearing and is now annoying). Become aware of everything that it brings up—

thoughts, justifications, emotions, or body sensations—and now say to yourself: "Interesting point of view I have that point of view," and take a deep breath. Repeat. "Interesting point of view I have that point of view."
And again!
"Interesting point of view I have that point of view." Breathe.
"Interesting point of view I have that point of view." Take another deep breath.
"Interesting point of view I have that point of view."

Now, is there a greater sense of space, peace and ease in your body and in your mind? If not, keep repeating the process. If you repeat it enough times your point of view will dissipate into a space of allowance.

As you practice IPOV, let go of your points of view as the only truth, and begin to step into the space of allowance, you may notice your body will begin to relax. Your triggers are created based on the significance of rightness or wrongness (felt by the body as an energetic "charge") that you give your and other people's points of view. Using this tool, you may even begin to notice how vested you are in holding onto your point of view as "right." That's ok. You can use IPOV for your desire to be right too! Using IPOV, eventually you eliminate the trigger button all together. You will still be aware of the behavior, but you are diffusing the energy you have placed on it and eventually the "button" becomes disconnected and no longer produces a reaction.

As you use this tool and step more into the space of allowance, you will also notice that the energy you used to project at your partner about your point of view begins to dissipate. Often just clearing your points of view of annoyance allows their behavior to change. They may even stop doing that behavior all together. Either way, you are no longer triggered.

From this space it is easier to look at your life from observation. When those IPOV's don't stick you anymore, you can ask some questions around what might work for you. This is where you can begin looking at what you would really like in your life, and what you'd like to change. You begin to *include* YOU in your choices, rather than excluding yourself to keep everyone else happy. You might be more willing to rock the boat and see what shows up. You may even begin the adventure of living. You may even start to enjoy it!

When you have taken the helm of the boat there is no fear, and a little rocking along the way is part of the fun. You can live each day as a continual, expansive adventure. "Who am I today, and what grand and glorious adventures will I have?®" When you are not divorcing you, you may find that you're more comfortable asking, "What else can I change?"

Keep doing this exercise for as many of your triggers as you can think of (including points of view other people have about you: "Interesting point of view *they* have that point of view"), creating more and more space for you and your partner.

Now you have the possibility of *being* the space of allowance, and when you ask a question from this space, you can begin to have so much more awareness than what your previously limited point of view would allow. For example, you could play with the question: "What would it take for our relationship to be much more kind, nurturing and supportive for both of us?" Then use the tool *Interesting Point of view* to clear the energy that comes up. Sit back and be amazed at what happens!

## What is a Point of View?—and
## how does it keep me wound up?

What is a point of view? Is it a judgment? No, but we turn it into judgment by making it right or wrong. If you are looking at your partner across the table, what you see around and behind him from your point of view will be different than what he sees around and behind you. Are you right? Is he wrong? Or is it just that his point of view originates from a different place? Once we have judged, it becomes solid and real to us. But remember, it started as just a view from a particular place. It was neither right nor wrong, good nor bad. Locking in judgment with your IPOV is what keeps you wound up.

*Would you be willing to get up and sit next to your partner and see things from their point of view, then reverse it and let them see things from yours?*

What if you were willing to look at and listen as objectively as possible to your partner and allow yourself to see from their point of view? If you gave each other this gift, is it possible that your communication might be easier?

By letting go of your judgments, you might even start to see what's right about you, and maybe even your partner, that you haven't been getting! If you could see them in a kinder light, would you be able to treat them kinder too? Remember how you treated each other in the beginning when you got together? If you weren't pointing fingers and judging one another, would that contribute to making either the choice for breaking up or continuing the relationship easier? (Keep in mind that letting go of judgment of them does not mean you have to stay with them, it just means that you can honor them, *and yourself*, by treating each other respectfully even through a breakup).

Still, whether you choose to stay or go, you've acknowledged that you'd like to change things. What would your choices look like without the trauma and drama of making each other wrong? If you were to let go of the rightness of your points of view and choose to have allowance for each other, what would that create?

## Will this work for me?—what kept you entangled once you got together

Allowance is allowing the person to be who they are, just as they are, and not needing to change them. Having allowance for you might be realizing that something doesn't work for you, and that you can be in allowance while still having the courage and the conviction to live the life you desire.

So let's look at who you are in relationship with: Are you looking at the person who is there, or are you wanting them to be someone else? How many of you choose "fixer-uppers" as partners, hoping that when you're done with the project, you'll be happy? Is that kind? To you? Or to them?

So will this relationship, with your partner exactly as they are right now, *work for you*? Notice I'm not asking "How can you make your relationship work?" The latter takes all the fun out of it and turns it into a job. This is one of those "deeper questions" I referred to earlier. Are you willing to have the courage to consider this question: *If you knew that your partner were never really going to be different from who they are now, would that work for you?!* Or would that *be work* for you?

One way to gain **clarity** for yourself about whether your relationship could work for you is to make a list of the things you require and desire in a relationship. For me, I want someone who is present with his body, who has a nurturing touch, who receives as well as gifts to me, who is kind and generous, fun and funny, who is aware, gives me space, is active, has his own interests, is adventurous, and enjoys good food. These are some of the qualities I desire in a relationship partner.

Before I was married, I didn't have this tool, so while I may have desired my husband to be like this, he actually was not. He was intellectual, much more in his head than present with his body. Although he seemed kind initially, he always had to point out where people were wrong–especially me. He would push the rightness of his point of view and have very little receptivity to others' ideas. He was usually serious and stood on moral high ground, but would joke around at the expense of someone else. He was controlling and didn't allow me much space to be alone. Even though he did have lots of interests of his own, we always did everything together; he didn't "go out with the guys" nor did he want me going out with the girls.

Since I had decided that he was my best friend and I loved spending all of my time with him, I cut off my awareness to the elements I really desired in a relationship. Finally being willing to look at the qualities that he embodied, as well as what I desired, made it clear why things were not easy between us.

Consider what qualities you desire and require in your relationship/partner, as well as what qualities you'd rather not have. I invite you to journal below:

Qualities I desire in a partner:

1. _____

2. _____

3. _____

4. _____

5. _____

6. _____

7. _____

8 _____

9. _____

10. _____

Qualities I'd rather not have in a partner:

1. _____

2. _____

3. _____

4. _____

5. _____

6. _____

7. _____

8 _____

9. _____

10. _____

Now look at your partner's basic nature. Do they match enough of the items on your list to make the relationship work for you? Can they change? Or would it be unkind to ask them to change to meet your needs? Would it actually be kinder to move on? And... What else is possible?®

## Your Point of View creates your Reality— untangling your reality from your joint reality

Have you ever noticed that you are usually right when it comes to your IPOV? For example, if you have a point of view that "all the good ones are taken," each person you meet is either not that great or already married. If you think men always cheat, or women are bitches, or relationships are hard work, then you can't have ease in relationships. If you think things never work out, then you are correct, they won't.

The funny thing is that *your point of view creates your reality,* your reality doesn't create your point of view—meaning that if you didn't have a point of view at the start, things could show up in a multitude of ways.

Every point of view we have limits us tremendously. When you start to realize that you can keep your IPOV's or clear them, you become more empowered to create the reality you'd really like to be living. When you don't limit your reality with rigid points of view, you can have the curiosity that creates an amazing adventure of greater possibilities everyday... every ten minutes!

All of our lives we are taught that curiosity and change are wrong. To fit in we have to try to get relationship/marriage right, work on it, stick with it (never change), and judge everything that doesn't fit into what we've decided is normal. Wow, that's a lot of work! No wonder we are tired, stressed, and not having fun! What would it be like to have the freedom that having curiosity with points of view would gift you? Tool #2 IPOV will assist with creating that.

## What if nothing you have ever chosen was wrong?—untangling from right and wrong

What if there is no such thing as right or wrong? Right or wrong is just judgment, another interesting point of view creating your reality that you can now change using these tools. But we were taught to navigate this life using judgement, to do good and get things right. Navigating based on judgment keeps you always looking for what's right, making it difficult to choose anything for fear that you'll be wrong. How often do you feel wrong, or feel stuck because you don't want to choose wrong? *What if you are not wrong? What if nothing you have ever chosen was wrong?* When I ask you that, does it make you feel lighter? That's because it is true. (We'll go deeper into this with Tool #6).

So what if nothing you have ever chosen was wrong? Each choice we make creates awareness. Some choices are not in our best interest. Sometimes you make a choice and get an immediate heavy feeling, which is an awareness, such as mailing out your wedding invitations and noticing a pit in your stomach as you head to the mailbox. Continuing along that path, knowing that it feels heavy might give you a clue that you could be headed for disaster. We tend to avoid our awareness instead of considering that changing our mind before popping those invitations in the mail could save years of unhappiness. Refraining from locking your choice into judgment (right or wrong, good or bad) allows you to choose again. And again, and again.

## Fairytales and Fantasy

How much of your relationship is based on the fantasy of what you wanted it to be?—the fantasy of what an ideal marriage is; the fantasy of who your partner is; the fantasy of what you wanted your life to be... Where did these come from? We pluck all that nonsense out of story books, and from the needs, wants and desires that other people project and expect. So where are YOU in all of that? What is it you'd really like? The problem with fantasy is that it is an ideal that we put into the future that can never actually be created. And we don't realize that we lose our awareness of what we would truly like to create when we have these fantasies in place.

So, how many fantasies do you have creating the romantic "dramady" of your relationship? Do you recall when the relationship "was over" for you? (Some of us knew *before* we got married!) And did you push that out of your awareness because it didn't match your fantasy? So how much of the relationship now is based on non-truths and ideals? Are you willing to let all of that go now, and start creating something else? *Interesting point of view I have all those points of view...* breathe, relax, repeat...

As you begin choosing more and more of what is true for you, the fantasies start falling away and the beauty of the real you begins to shine through. *You may be startled by how many of the things in your life are not things you would choose for yourself!*

Once you come out of the fantasy you can look at what you require. What if YOU are all you need? What would it be like to have your own back? What would it be like to commit to your life? Will you be there for you? When you are, anyone else becomes an addition to your life, because you are complete, as you, first. Are you willing to choose to commit to your life? Let's begin with unwinding what is *not* you, and allow the *true* you to emerge. This brings us to our next tool.

## Tool #3: The Bars

One of the foundational tools of Access Consciousness for unwinding the body and the mind is the Bars. This self-care treatment has the remarkable effect of clearing your mind and creating space and peace in your body because it dissipates clogged energy. We call it "running Bars." It consists of lying back and relaxing as your facilitator gently touches varying combinations of the 32 points on your head that release thousands of judgments, limitations, and decisions that keep you from being present. It's like defragging your brain. Just like your computer, your brain stores all kinds of junk, and it needs regular maintenance and dumping of the trash bin to function at its highest capacity.

If you are feeling stressed, have lots of mind chatter, low energy, etc. go and get your Bars run! It will assist your body in relaxing, your mind in getting clear and peaceful, and your capacity to be the space of interesting point of view with greater ease because when you discharge the physiological component of your points of view (held in your body), it's like choosing a new path—not just that those old ruts and bumps aren't there anymore, but that you can take a whole different road!

Throughout our process of divorce, every time I faced something that made me feel heavy, contracted, or something that I thought I couldn't deal with, I used IPOV and got my Bars run. Like when we were going through the storage closets, or looking at our finances, or even contemplating how to tell our friends and family... all the heaviness that came up would melt away during the Bars session. It gave me the space to unwind and afterward I was able to easily handle everything that came my way.

Journal entry—written in 2016

*Now it has been over six years since our divorce and while things are sometimes difficult, I have tools to help me. I do my best to just be aware of what will work, not making him wrong or right, and asking questions to facilitate more ease for myself and the kids. "What else is possible here?"*

*When difficulties come up, my favorite tool is getting my Bars run. Access Bars always helps to free me from the stuck feeling of no choice. It clears away the upset so I can deal with the situation from a space of observation, rather than judgment.*

If you had no solidified points of view you actually would be able to have total freedom and choice. Does that sound like something you'd like to have? I highly recommend you have your Bars run.

Contact me and I will be happy to guide you to a practitioner. You will be glad you did.

For those times that having a Bars session is not possible, I created an audio called Unwinding, which is like a guided meditation (see appendix III for a link to download). Listening to this audio will create space, relaxation, and help you unwind. You can even "loop" it on very low volume while you sleep to create deeper clearing. Or try using this audio in conjunction with all these other tools to assist in creating space to reclaim YOU!

# Step 2

# Dissolving Past Trauma

## Freedom to be you

Have you ever noticed how your mind can take hold of an event in the past and you can spend hours thinking about it, reliving it over again and again, trying to figure out why what happened happened, and what you could have done differently? It all feels so heavy and it becomes hard to get up in the morning. **When you walk through the past in your mind, you are actually projecting all of that energy into your future again.** Not your best choice.

How do you get out of this habitual pattern? For some, the pattern is so ingrained that they aren't even aware of what they're doing. Letting go of the past was not easy for me... that is until I learned to apply this tool that literally erased all the ties, significances, and holding patterns that kept me captive.

## Tool #4: Uncreate and destroy all your Points of Creation & Points of Destruction (POC & POD) to erase the past

You are the creator of everything in your life. This should come as a relief because it means that you can uncreate things as well. This tool is incredibly helpful for clearing out hidden limiting beliefs, attitudes, judgments and decisions that keep us from having clarity, and the ability to choose that which will give us what we desire in life. With these beliefs and decisions in place, we end up destroying ourselves and our future possibilities. This tools is called POC & POD and it is like a magic wand that releases the energetic ties to all those beliefs, including the ones we're not even aware of. Whereas "interesting point of view" deals with the points of view you are aware of, POC & POD reaches deeper into the past, into all the nooks and crannies where you've hidden your own knowing from yourself.

"POC" stands for Point of Creation which takes you to the exact moment in time/space where you put that limitation into place, and erases it. "POD" stands for Point of Destruction, which begins dissolving everywhere you began (and still are) destroying yourself in order to keep that conclusion in place. Together, they untangle you from the awareness and choices you've made that are keeping you from making new ones.

Using this tool is called *running a process*. Einstein's work revealed that what we perceive as solid matter is mostly empty space with a pattern of energy running through it. Running a process can change the energy, which changes physical reality. The way it works is you ask a question to bring up the energy of where you are stuck and then simply say, "POC & POD all that!" You don't even have to have a cognitive idea about what that energy is. Your choice to let it go is more powerful than the significance you once gave it.

For example, call up in your awareness the idea of divorcing your partner. What beliefs do you have about divorce? You may have some specific words come to mind. But most likely, your predominant awareness is beyond your mind. It might be fear, or a heavy feeling in your body or tightness in your neck and shoulders. The energetics that create that body feeling are all the polarities of your beliefs/decisions/judgments, known and unknown. So get a sense of that feeling, and just say, *Ok! I uncreate everything that is, and destroy everything that keeps me holding onto any of those limitations.* POC & POD. Breathe... let it go.

When you ask to uncreate everything you made significant around a particular event, belief, judgment or thought, and destroy the limitations you have placed on yourself—"POC & POD!"—it actually disappears from your reality, layer by layer, and anyone else who is connected to you that has that same limitation can change too. When the energy releases, the physical limitation can change, or even disappear. So you ask the questions, say "POC & POD," allow the energy to shift, and you start to get free. And as an added bonus, your family, friends and people around might start to change too!! It's a beautiful side effect.

When can you use POC and POD? Anytime! You can ask questions to unlock yourself from the belief systems and judgments that you have learned, and change the energy in your life so that you don't function from the same limitations any longer. This is like nothing you've ever heard of... and everything you've always known was possible, but haven't quite had access to.

## Come out of fixing the past—allowing the real you to emerge

How many of the problems you have had in your marriage are simply a continuation of some conflict that occurred in the past? You're still trying to figure out the solution. You're still blaming the other person for it. You can't seem to let go of it and move beyond. How can you keep looking behind you at the past and expect your future to be any different?

So the pain of a breakup keeps going forward because nobody's creating a different future; everybody's trying to solve the past. The past is not solvable, it's over! If you don't look toward what you would like to create, you will fixate on all the problems and loop back again and again on the wrongness of each other. This doesn't work. Letting go of the emotional charge from past experiences allows you to see your future choices more clearly. So, if you POC & POD as much as you can about the past, you clear the way to move forward. You can even POC & POD your relationship!

Why would you want to do that? If you POC & POD your relationship, it allows you to be more present and create your relationship *new* each day. When you uncreate and destroy the limitations of your relationship and everything it has been, you are freed to create something new, with or without your partner. Imagine if you could wipe the slate clean each day, no more built up resentments, just the two of you refreshed and new. How much more would you enjoy your life? How does this work? Each morning, say I *uncreate and destroy everything my relationship was before today*, POC & POD. Then move into question.

Questions take you out of judgment and into creation. When you ask your partner: "What do you want to create with this relationship?", it gently moves them out of their judgments and gets them to look at your future choices. Each choice you make creates new awareness. When you move into **question**, you can begin looking at what future possibilities you would like to create.

"What else might be possible here?" "What would we actually like to create?" and "What can we do different?" POC & POD *and Question* are the first steps in creating yourself outside of the mess of your current entangled relationship.

During my breakup I started clearing out limiting beliefs, attitudes, judgments and decisions that kept me from having clarity and the ability to create what I'd like to have in life by unwinding (IPOV and Bars Sessions), letting go of past problems by wiping the slate clean each day (POC & POD), and moving forward to create something different (Question: What will this choice create?).

When you incorporate these tools, you might find that you actually like each other. You might have a change of heart and become open to the possibilities of a future together that might actually work for you both. Or you might become clear that the future is creating your lives separately. **Only you will know** what is true and correct for you. Trust yourself. Be true to you.

## The Back Door—if your back door is open, are you really "here" for yourself or your partner?

Do you have a back door in your relationship? Is there a deal-breaking point or line that, if crossed, ends the relationship for you? Most people have their back door open in their relationships. They have expectations, that if not met, means they're gone—out the back door. It's as if they're poised and ready to run when that metaphorical line is crossed. With this underlying point of view, can you see how you are setting your relationship up for an eventual end?

What does this look like? Rather than facing issues and dealing with each other in a kind and caring way, you compile your judgments and unfulfilled requirements until you finally feel justified in leaving.

What would it be like to have no requirements of your partner, only requirements of yourself? Do you know what it feels like to have someone require things of you, even though they don't articulate what they are? There is an energy projected at you that makes you feel like you're not doing enough, not doing the right thing, somehow letting them down, or feeling totally controlled. It is a terrible feeling.

So what if rather than requiring and projecting things at your partner, you requested instead? "Darling, would you be willing to do _____ for me?" That way they have choice to do it or not do it. There is no projection and subsequent resentment if it is resisted or rejected silently. Are you willing to ask for what you'd like? Give them choice? And know that you have choice too? Can you be in allowance of their choices, and have gratitude for them being in your life?

## Tool #5: Where there is gratitude, there is no room for judgment

Judgment is an ugly killer leaving nothing but despondency and feelings of separation in its wake. But, gratitude dissolves and dissipates judgment; it is like a gentle, nurturing wave of beauty and goodness. Gratitude is a generative energy. It *creates more* of what you are grateful for. So what would it take to live from awareness and gratitude for what *is*, instead of holding onto judgment? I don't mean to say that having gratitude means you're going to be delighted with every little thing, but I do mean that by having gratitude for your partner, you begin to see what's right about the things you had made wrong.

Have gratitude for the things they do (or did) so more of that ease can show up. Maybe you enjoy the way she takes care of certain things for you, or that he handles messy situations. My husband used to do some of the grocery shopping and he dealt with the plumbing issues. When you can see the upside, you can have possibilities continually emerge. Your life would be filled with ease and kindness rather than blame and negativity.

Having gratitude, even during the breakup, allowed us to move through the process so much quicker with less stress. When we put our house on the market we worked as a team, having gratitude for the house and what it would be contributing to our futures. Our realtor couldn't believe that we were divorcing. Our energy was so different than most other couples in this situation. Our house sold within a week of listing at full asking price.

## Feelings of Failure

One of the many emotions that comes up when contemplating a breakup is failure. You look at your relationship as a failure if it ends in divorce. Whose point of view is that? Is it yours? Is it historical, cultural or societal? Do you have memories of gossip and and stories about how terrible it was that other families were splitting up? Those memories might not be in the front of your mind, but the energetic imprint they left on you still rules! When the feeling of failure shows up for you, **POC & POD** it! You literally just notice how you feel, and ask to uncreate and destroy everything creating limitations for you and your body. Erasing the past can really be that simple! If you choose to use this tool, you will get free of those chains that kept you down.

## Clearing the Physical Past—cultivating space for you

Uncreating your relationship every day can also be applied to your belongings. *I uncreate and destroy my relationship with all of my belongings, POC & POD.* This will be helpful when going through the closets, basement, attic and garage as it can bring up a lot of heavy energy. All of those places where we have stored things, all the meaning, memories and significance attached to those things, can make it difficult to sort through and move beyond. So uncreating your relationship, and your relationship to things, before you begin clearing your physical past can begin to diffuse the emotional attachment.

Every time I attempted to go through the storage we had collected, I was almost knocked out by the heavy, dizzying energy that accompanied it. Have you noticed this phenomenon for yourself? We would start looking through boxes of storage stuff, and this energy would come over me. I would feel more and more tired, like Dorothy in the field of poppies! If it's possible to just walk out of the room and go lie down for a few minutes, that can help. In addition to destroying and uncreating my relationships, what really cleared the fog was using Tool #3 as much as possible: having an Access Bars session. Bars, in conjunction with POC &

POD, reaches deeper into your unconsciousness **and your body** to clear out sticky limitations and cultivate space for you.

Fortunately, my husband and I both had been trained to run Bars and often would work on each other—even during our breakup. What a gift that was! After the session we both felt completely renewed, like our batteries were fully charged, and the slate had been wiped clean. We felt a sense of space, clarity of mind, and a fullness of peace. It was almost as if we were going through someone else's stuff... there was so little attachment to the piles.

Have you noticed how easy it is to go through someone else's stuff? That's because you have no vested interest in those things, no story behind them, no significance attached. Some people call it Zen, the art of un-attachment, and it can take years of meditation to achieve it... or you could have an hour Bars session and *become it*.

Once you have sorted and cleared out the closets you will likely have a huge sense of relief. You may even feel energized and excited to continue your journey. There will be space for you to relax; space to rearrange; space to add new belongings. You might like to redecorate, or get some new outfits, and start stepping into being more of YOU.

# Step 3

## Navigation System

### Clarity for your future

How do you figure out what to do? Most of us grew up learning that we should figure out what we should do using logic, reason, and linear thinking. But that's what got us into this mess in the first place. And that's a lot of "shoulds" which do not necessarily match what we truly desire. What else is possible then? What about those moments that you've had that you call *serendipity*?! You know how you whimsically choose to do something and the most magical connections get created and you have an amazing day?! Well, what if you could create your entire life to feel like that? What if it is possible to learn how to "follow the energy" which is really what sparks serendipitous events in the first place? Letting go of linear, logical thinking, and instead following the energy, gives you a sense of lightness, freedom and clarity about your choices.

As I mentioned before, my husband and I did everything together. We worked together, ate meals together, shopped together, slept in the same bed, traveled together... And for a long time I was ok with that. I had gotten used to this way of life. Then some things came up that began shifting this "always together" pattern. There were a few times that I needed to travel on my own, to work at a trade show, or to return home to the East Coast for a funeral. I started to notice that as soon as I walked through security in the airport I felt different. I was no longer all the labels—mom, wife, partner—I was me. It was as if I could breathe deeper, spread my wings, drop the pretense, and just be myself. It was a sense of fun and ease and adventure that I had long ago given up... but here it was again!

*What would it take to have this sense of self always? Everything that doesn't allow that, I uncreate and destroy it, POC & POD. Breathe...*

If I were truly being me, what would I choose? What would I like? Who would I be? It had always been easy for me to perceive what other people wanted, what they required, and how I could provide or be what was necessary for them; but I had no idea what I wanted.

When you are in a long term relationship, often you have given up your dreams and desires for the union, or what your partner wants, or what you *think* your partner wants that might not actually be true. When the two of you become one, what often happens is you lose your awareness of YOU. You lose your awareness of where you'd like to go and what you'd like to do. You give in to the maintenance of the relationship and forget self. Who's driving the boat? Who's looking at the big picture and where are you going?

As I contemplated what I really wanted in life, I realized that I needed to learn a **navigation system**—tools that would allow me to move in the direction that I'd like my life to go. I realized that it was truly vital to me that I continually grow so I wouldn't stagnate and get bored, or find myself lost when the kids left the nest. I looked at how much of my life was a fantasy based on other people's ideas and beliefs of what is the best in this reality.

Born in Boston, MA, I had a traditional upbringing where education, family, and conforming to the norm was expected and highly valued. Somehow I came away with this dream of perfectly fitting into what was expected of me, while having a few crumbs of what was really true for me tucked into the corners somewhere. My childhood fantasy was to live in a house with a white picket fence in Vermont or Connecticut, and have a family. And while I can remember wanting that for my future, I also noticed how it had no energy to it. It wasn't really *my* dream! It was more likely something I picked up from a childhood book, a movie I had seen, or from friends and peers around me.

Over the summer when I was thirteen I traveled across the United States from Massachusetts to California, where I fell in love with San Francisco. I returned home full of excitement about the possibilities of someday living there. When I told my family about my dreams, they laughed and thought I was silly. Regardless of what they thought, secretly I knew that's what I wanted for myself.

When something is true for you there is an energy present. It feels expansive, exciting, generative, and can make you smile, giggle or feel happy. You recognize this energy more as you begin to trust yourself and follow its *lightness*.

On the other hand, when something is not true for you it can feel heavy, contracted, twisted; like a kick in the gut, or a squeezing off in the throat. Each of us has our own way of sensing what is heavy and what is light. In the beginning it may just be a wisp of an awareness—a feather touch. *Pay attention!* Learn to follow that feather touch, as this will strengthen your ability to sense these energies more dynamically.

## Navigation through sensing what is expansive—following the energy

### Tool #6: If it's Light, it is true; If its Heavy, its a lie.

Choose light, and your life will become more expansive than you can imagine. Choose heavy and it will become more dense and contracted. Simply follow your awarenesses toward the lightness, rather than choosing the heaviness, and you'll create your future with lightness, expansiveness and aliveness. This is called following the energy.

As I mentioned earlier, the way your body gives you the awareness of light and heavy is unique to you, so by playing with this tool you'll begin to sense the ways that it tells you what is light and what is heavy. Sometimes "light" will make you smile, giggle, laugh out loud, or just feel like your heart opens. And sometimes "heavy" can feel like a pit in your stomach, a sinking feeling, depression, or tightness somewhere in your body. And some choices feel flat—no energy either direction. Play with some questions and start to sense what is light and heavy for you. Doing so will begin to strengthen that muscle of awareness.

For example, a friend was headed home from work and felt a heaviness when she began to go the "normal" way home. So she turned off the main route and took the back road instead. When she got home she learned of a major accident on the freeway that had stopped traffic for hours. Her sensing the heaviness, and choosing the lighter route, avoided the possibility of being in the accident or stuck in a traffic jam.

Most people choose what feels heavy, because they think that the feeling of solidity means it's real. When you choose something that is heavy for you it almost always leads to more difficulty and unhappiness because you are going against an awareness that something supportive of you is possible. Once you learn to recognize what *light* is like for you, begin to make choices that are congruent with this lightness and aliveness. This allows you to navigate based on an **energetic awareness** of what your choices will create in the future. Don't take my word for it... try it out for a while and see what greater, more joyful possibilities you can create!

Are you ready to ask some questions and start applying this tool?

*Has your relationship run its course?* Yes or No? Rather than going into judgment about what is right or wrong, try looking at what is light or heavy. If Yes feels lighter, then perhaps it is time to move on. You've likely had some wonderful times, some memorable times, and some difficult times too. What if you didn't need to make the relationship *all* bad to move on? What if you still love and care about your spouse, you just can't live with them? Does that feel light? If so, then it's true for you. Continue to ask questions and sense what makes you feel lighter.

## What is Being Selfish?—gain clarity about who you are choosing for

In society, the idea of selflessness rules; and doing anything for yourself is *selfish!* It is bad and wrong! What if that isn't actually correct? It feels really heavy to me.

Let's look at the definition of the word selfish, per my 1934 Webster's New International Dictionary: "Caring for oneself; regarding one's own comfort; in disregard or at the expense of others." The last part feels heavy to me. You've heard the old adage *If Mama ain't happy, ain't nobody happy*, right? So what if we incorporated the first part and started *including* ourselves? What if including you in your life, in your choices, is actually a greater contribution to those around you and the world? *What if including you doesn't have to be at the expense of others?* Does that feel light? What if everything that we have been told is a wrongness in this reality is actually a *strongness* that we have been unwilling to be? Would you be willing to be that now by starting to include you?

For example, a client was feeling very upset and contracted because people close to her, including her family, were judging her as being selfish and creating problems in her marriage. As she was speaking the words, each time she came to a judgment of herself it felt so heavy she could barely get the words out. So I asked her, "Does that feel light when you say that?" She said, "No." Sniff, sniff. Remember: sensing heaviness means you are aware of a lie. So, what if you trusted your awareness of what is true for you, no matter what?

She also mentioned that she felt wrong for dressing up, looking pretty, and being happy. She said it made her feel insane. That is correct! In this reality, being average, dressing down, wearing sweatpants and being unhappy (especially during a breakup) are what is normal and sane. So I asked her: "Are you willing to be out of touch with this reality, and be insanely happy?!" That created such lightness in her world she burst out laughing.

Only from this space of lightness can we create and generate, change, choose, and Be. So whatever you do, don't play with the heavy/light tool to navigate your choices... It might just assist in creating a lot more ease and possibilities!

Trusting your own awareness, even when others don't agree, strengthens that muscle we've been talking about. You need to learn to trust *you*. Standing strong in your own awareness, with no need to resist any judgment, or align and agree, begins to create an energy of true confidence to BE you. Only *you* know what is true for you. When you have trust in you, you step into fully Being You, and can begin creating the life you'd love to be living.

The next morning I got a text from my client that said: "Thank you Julie! The energy has changed. What will it take to be the resonance of me with no apology? So grateful!"

Are you willing to have things change this quickly and easily? Is now the time to start creating the life you'd love to be living?

Rather than contracting when faced with adversity—expand! Turn it up! Step into more. When you contract you begin to cut off your awareness, your ability to ask questions and choose for you. Turning it up allows you to have more awareness to choose what is actually true for you. And please recognize that when someone accuses you of something, it is just their interesting point of view (not real or true) that they're perpetrating on you in an attempt to manipulate you into choosing something more comfortable for *them*. If it feels heavy to you, it's incongruent with *you*. Period. What is true for you will always make you feel lighter.

## Acknowledge how aware you are already

One of the keys that I teach in my personal development classes is how most of us are way more aware than we have acknowledged. We are like satellite dishes with hundreds of channels receiving information from thousands of miles away. So, what if ninety eight percent of your thoughts, feelings and emotions actually don't belong to you? What do I mean by that and how could that be possible?

Well, from a quantum physics perspective, we are made up of pure energy. Even our cells—better yet, our atoms—are just energy. So even though we don't often sense this on a cognitive level, we're subtly aware of the energies all around us all the time. Consider the probably countless times you've come home from work and could sense that your partner was upset with you. You can feel that energy from across the room, maybe even from across town! So even though this concept might be far-fetched to your mind, doesn't it make you feel lighter just reading that? If it does, then it is true for you.

But, you aren't only aware of your partner's energy. You are aware of everyone and everything around you! Most of us don't realize that other people affect us because there is no measurable way of proving it; instead, we attribute our irritability in traffic to our own time crunch, instead of acknowledging that we're likely picking up on that energy from everyone else in the traffic jam too! You can tune into this drama, and be totally entertained, preoccupied, distracted... or you can realize that *practically none* of it is yours.

*What if you were to acknowledge that you are way more psychic than you have given yourself credit for?*

When you acknowledge these thoughts, feelings, and emotions as your *awareness* and not *you*, you can let them fall away more easily. When you stop buying into them as you or your story, you also stop using them to defend your rightness or not-wrongness to your partner.

Imagine how much easier life would be, not just in your marriage, but at work and with friends, if you didn't have to buy into everything you were aware of? How much less would you and your partner fight? When you begin to acknowledge what isn't yours, *you begin to know that you know.* You don't have to get bogged down by every thought, feeling or emotion, so you end up having more energy. This gives you much more possibility. It also strengthens your trust in yourself.

As an example, a friend was heading home and started to feel upset, but she had had a great day so she became curious about what was going on. As she pulled into the driveway she noticed her husband's truck parked at an awkward angle that made it difficult for her to park. Rather than compounding the upset by being mad at him for parking poorly, she went in to see what happened during his day at work. She *knew* that he was probably angry or upset, so she was sure to approach with sensitivity and caring. Her kindness diffused his anger. When you know your partner is upset, do you add fuel to the fire? Do you think to yourself, "He is always stressed and angry!"

Remember, *your point of view creates your reality!* Not the other way around. So when you think, "He will never change," or "She always snaps about that," what are you creating with those IP-OV's? How often is it even your point of view anyway?! Which brings me to the next tool that helps you become aware of how aware you are.

## Tool #7: Ask, "Is this mine, someone else's, or something else?" and return it all to sender

What if we all are far more aware than we have ever acknowledged? Some of us are so sensitive that a normal volume of two or three is like hearing a speaker on volume 20. And some people perceive information from a distance of eight miles to 8,000 miles away! Although you may try, you can't turn off your awareness. So, how do you deal with this information so that it doesn't hinder your ability to enjoy living? Using this tool can assist. Remember, what if ninety eight percent of the thoughts, feelings and emotions you have have nothing to do with you? Imagine the relief of not having to process all of that stuff anymore!

How does it work? For every thought, feeling and emotion you have, ask, *"Is this mine, someone else's, or something else?"* If you sense even a flash of lightness or space when you ask this question, that's your "light" indicator. When you ask, you may notice things lighten up at "someone else's" so everything you thought was yours, just *return to sender.*

If it lightens up at "something else," ask if it is an awareness of the earth. Lots of people are sensitive to the changes on Earth and when they acknowledge it, and give that energy to the earth, their pain or symptoms dissipate. For instance, many women who get hot flashes think they are having normal menopausal symptoms, however when I ask them the question, and it lightens up on "something else's" and they give that energy to the earth, all the symptoms go away. They can then ask themselves each time they feel that energy coming on. It is empowering to know how sensitive we are, and that we can contribute to each other and the planet using this tool.

One of my clients was complaining that her entire body was hurting from a big hike she had taken earlier that day. She was not a particularly sporty person, so it made sense to her that she was feeling the pain. When I asked her: "Is that yours, someone else's, or something else?" she gasped, and started jumping up and down with glee. It was not *hers*! The pain had totally disappeared in that moment just by asking the question!

For every thought, feeling or emotion, keep asking yourself: "Is this mine, someone else's or something else?" Acknowledge that it's not yours, and keep returning it to sender. Returning all of the worry and fear that you perceive, rather than buying it as yours, will totally change your life! If you use this tool for three days you will have a sense of total peace in your mind and body.

Let's practice using this tool now. Take a moment and think about leaving your relationship. Notice what comes up when you are considering your breakup? Do you feel anxiety, fear, or guilt? Or do you want to avoid thinking about it because as soon as you do you're hit with a tsunami of thoughts of fear and anxiety?—none of which may belong to you. Now, all of the thoughts that are coming in, ask: "Is this mine? Someone else's? Or something else?" Take a breath. Notice what changes in your body. If it lightens up even a little, it's not yours. You don't even have to know where it came from. Ask to return everything to sender with consciousness attached and then POC & POD everything you thought was yours that isn't. Now sense the freedom that shows up in your mind and body. (You may have to repeat several times).

Here are a couple more examples to illustrate this tool:

A friend was heading into the city with her husband for an evening out on the town. She was excited and looking forward to their date night. Having lived in the city years before, she longed for some of those experiences that their quaint home in the country lacked. As they got in the car and headed south, all of a sudden she felt anxiety come up and start to take over her. She thought, *I love the city, why would I feel anxiety?* So rather than buying it as hers, she played with this tool and asked where it was coming from, someone else or something else? As she contemplated this for a moment, all of those feelings of anxiety subsided and she was back to excitement. You don't necessarily have to say, "return to sender," sometimes just asking the question allows things to shift and change.

Another client mentioned that he was having difficulty feeling confident when dating, but said he usually doesn't have issues with confidence. I asked him some questions to find out what was going on. Last time he had a date, he got ready to leave his house feeling great, but as soon as he got to the door to pick up his date he was suddenly nervous and unsure. While he was relaying the information I noticed that there was a twisted energy coming up, so I asked him if what he was feeling was actually *his*. No. He had this huge "aha" moment, which helped him realize that he was picking up on her feelings (and possibly anyone else who has ever been nervous for a date before!) Acknowledging this awareness brought such a relief. He felt so much lighter (recognizing what was really true for him). We receive the information so quickly that we think it is ours, but what if it is actually an *awareness*?

Once you clear away the thoughts and feelings that are not yours, you are better able to handle the ones that *are* yours. Anything that is left over, you can use the tools IPOV and POC & POD to continue to unwind.

This may seem like a stretch, but I promise if you commit to using this tool for at least three days, at the end of those three days your head will be totally clear, calm and quiet. You will have an awareness of yourself and others and the clarity to know the difference. You become like a walking, talking meditation, and you will have way more space and peace in your world. You might even begin to feel happy. Imagine that?!

When you begin asking, "Is this mine?" you find out that almost everything you thought was yours belongs to other people. How many times have you thought something, and the opposite was actually true? When you hear something and it feels really heavy, you think it must be true because it feels so real. However the tool, "If its light its right, and if its heavy its a lie," indicates the opposite! How much have we had everything upside down and not working, and what would it take to undo that? This brings us to the next tool.

## Tool #8: Everything is the opposite of what it appears to be, and nothing is the opposite of what it appears to be

This tool is great for those times when you are in your head, twisting yourself up about something, and can't seem to stop thinking in circles. In Access Consciousness it is lovingly called

"The Crazy Phrase," because when you are feeling crazy you can repeat it and it magically shuts off your crazy mind.

For example, you may be thinking that your partner is cheating on you when they are on a business trip, so you get all worked up when they head out of town. Your mind races in circles, creating things that may not be true. For instance, you create in your head them meeting for drinks, their eyes locking, and hushed conversation. You can't seem to get away from it. It affects your whole day, your body, your sleeping patterns. You can't eat. You feel sick. The difficulty here is that you are in your head, and therefore not in your awareness (possibly even your awareness... of someone else's worries!) What if none of these events actually occurred? This phrase is like a switch that gets you out of being stuck in your mind, unlocks the spinning, and allows you to gain space to see things from another perspective.

*Everything is the opposite of what it appears to be, and nothing is the opposite of what it appears to be.* (repeat 3 - 10 times to stop the spinning)

Where else does this apply? Many people talk about simplifying their lives. What if we would be better served adding more to our lives, rather than focusing and narrowing down? I'll give you an example: When my kids were little and attending Montessori School, they had classical music on in the background during class. When they came home to do homework I noticed that having a quiet place with no distractions actually made it more difficult for them to complete their assignments. They said it was boring, and I noticed if they had on a movie with no sound, and the radio playing music and people talking in the background it was much easier to get everything done.

What if we really function better when we do more, rather than less? What if everything is the opposite of what we've been conditioned to believe? Just like how I realized that I enjoyed having some alone time and the space to do my own thing, instead of doing everything with my husband. So rather than taking things at face value, what if we were to use Tool #1 here to lower our barriers and look honestly at our desires, and then asked a question that might lend more clarity as to what we want? Looking at life from a different place can allow so much more to open up.

Often times, our automatic response when faced with something intense like anger or overwhelm, is to contract. We get small, cut off our potency, our awareness, and therefore, our ability to change the situation. This really became clear to me the other night in a class I was facilitating. As I listened to my students, I began to sense that they would create this contraction when trying to understand their partner by going into their universe to look for clarity. I kept hearing them say things like, "Why would he do that?" and "I just don't get it! I don't do that to her!" What I became aware of was that, in order to do this—to focus, and try and understand—we must out of necessity cut off any part of our own awareness or perception that is beyond what the other person is aware of, in order to fit through the doorway of their limited reality. Once inside, you begin to look around, but have lost your larger perspective. Can you see how this would lock you up? So *everywhere you've decided that understanding was a good idea, that it would give you clarity, and that you must contract yourself or your awareness when triggered, will you uncreate and destroy all of that?! POC & POD. Everything is the opposite of what it appears to be, and nothing is the opposite of what it appears to be. Breathe...*

*Interesting point of view I have all those points of view...* breathe, relax,

Let it go...

What if instead, when triggered, you realized you had a choice? What if you chose to expand? What if you chose to get curious? What if you maintained the space to observe what was going on without the need to go to judgment? What if *everything is the opposite of what it appears to be, and nothing is the opposite of what it appears to be?*

## Awareness of the Future—developing your ability to perceive energy in order to navigate toward your dreams

> "You have to be willing to look at your life with total honesty, and get clear on where you are, and where you'd like to go. This takes a tremendous amount of vulnerability and trust in yourself."
> - Gary Douglas

Being willing to look at your life with total honesty takes a tremendous amount of courage, as well as vulnerability and trust. It took time for me to be willing to have an awareness of the future. At first I didn't even want to look. Looking would crack open the possibility of total destruction of the facade I had built up as my perfect life. It took courage to even peek. So many times I would ask questions about my future, yet was not willing to trust myself.

I would cringe and shrink away from my own awareness. Here I was using the tools, but I wasn't willing to have my awareness.

So, I strengthened my trust over time with things I was willing to look at: simpler choices, like where to go for dinner, when to make sales appointments, or which airline tickets to book (with so many flight options, expanding my awareness into the future helped me navigate without going into my head).

When I was finally ready to look at breaking up, I began asking some deeper questions for each of us, and the kids... *What would our lives be like if I made this choice?*

Every time I asked the question and perceived the energy, I sensed such lightness and joy, and everyone's life expanding. I was shocked. Shouldn't it be the opposite? That's what we are taught to believe. How is it that divorce could be *light*?! It goes against normal, rational, societal ideas and beliefs of what is right. But it was so incredibly expansive, I had to pay attention. What if everything is the opposite of what it appears to be and nothing is the opposite of what it appears to be?

Again, what if choosing to end something was the best thing you could choose? What doors would open as a result of that choice? If you take it out of linear, logical thinking and look at the energy of it, choice becomes clear, quick and easy. And you can always choose again! After making a choice, if you get an additional awareness, you can then make another choice based on what you know now that you didn't before.

Would you like to know how to look into your future?

## Tool #9: Ask, "If I make this choice, what would my life be like in 5 years?"

Looking five years into the future doesn't mean you have to stick to that choice for five years. Locking it in would no longer be a choice, that would be a decision. A decision is where you solidify something and can't change it. Using this tool, you are looking at the energy of what that choice will create, even if it ends up being a temporary one. It is simply a way to gain awareness of the future.

Let's practice now: Get into a quiet space. Clear your mind of any IPOV, and ask, "If I make this choice _____ (fill in the blank), what will my life be in five years?" Notice what the energy feels like in your body. Just sense it and let it go. *Uncreate and destroy everything that was, POC & POD.*

Next, ask, "If I don't make this choice, what will my life be like in five years?" Perceive that; then release it. Let it go. If there is another possibility look at that energetically, then let it go.

Sense into the energy of each possibility, not thinking about what will look like, but sensing what it will feel like (it should only take you a few seconds). Some things may feel really heavy and contracted, perhaps in your throat or stomach. Some may feel really light and expansive, and open up your heart area, or your crown. Some may feel kind of flat. Choose the option that will be closest to what you'd like your life to *feel* like. I know, it sounds too simple, but you may be surprised what you can create by trusting your own knowing.

**Indulge your choice**—step into the possibility of choosing simply based on the *energetic awareness of lightness*. You don't need to say it out loud, or tell anyone what you are choosing. The thing is to start noticing what your choice options will create for your life–from your own awareness–and then make choices that support the most expansive outcome for you and everyone involved. This is how you build and strengthen your knowing.

Notes from interview with a friend:

GP kept hearing this knowing voice in the back of her mind that wouldn't go away. She had pulled the wool over her eyes so tight, but had come to the point that she couldn't keep it down any longer. Her relationship was not working for her. Her partner was totally dependent on her; he wanted to have sex all the time—but it was from a place of lack and proving that he was ok. It felt clingy and un-nurturing. She was constantly trying to pull him up to her level, and include him in all of her creative expressions and business opportunities; yet this slowed her down and kept things from blooming for her. She looked at the energy of her life, with brutal honesty, in several scenarios: If she left him, what would that generate in five years? If she stayed together, what would that be like in five years? When asking this question the energy became apparent, as was her choice: leaving the relationship would expand her life in about 3 months time. She noticed that exactly 3 months to the day from making this choice, her life did lighten up and expand, and continues to grow.

Trusting and acting on your awareness will give you a sense of confidence that you're creating something greater and more expansive in your life. You may not know what it will look like, because you are navigating by the energy. Most of the time it will look different than you think, but it will *feel* just like the awareness you had.

I made the choice to end my marriage, and now years later, I am amazed at how all of our lives have expanded. The children are happy, thriving, and know that they are loved by both of their parents. My world continues to grow as an artist and jeweler, and an Access Consciousness Certified Facilitator inspiring people all over the world. I have more energy, am happier, and look younger. If you would have told me that I'd be living in this beautiful home in Marin, have a retail boutique in Mill Valley, and be traveling teaching personal development classes, and coaching clients, I'm not sure I would have believed it was possible while being a single mom. The energy of my life feels more expansive than ever, very much like what I had sensed all those years ago.

I'm not saying that there haven't been difficulties along the road. There have been. But each time, I reach for the tools and work through these first 3 steps to unwind, dissipate past trauma, and realize that I can navigate with clarity. I also keep asking questions. *And now, what would I like to choose?*

# Step 4

## Breaking through Barriers

### What would you create if you could choose anything?

Part of the difficulty when considering a breakup is getting past the initial idea of living separately. We rely so much upon our spouse and our lives are so intertwined that sometimes it is hard to trust that you can be successful on your own. Many times we don't even recognize what the other person does for us, for the kids, or for the household until they are not there.

Living alone can come as a shock after so many years living together. All of a sudden you have all this time on your hands. While it may sound great in theory, it can be terrifying for some. When we are approaching our lives from a fearful place, we've already come to some conclusions about how something *is* or is *going to be.* Usually it has a negative slant. We can shift out of this by noticing what we're feeling, and then asking some questions that allow us to change the energy.

## Tool #10: Live in the Question

Ask questions, they open up possibilities. Answers close the door. Allow the questions to be. Don't try to get the answer. Don't try to figure anything out. Just ask, and let them to go out into the Universe and create possibilities for you. Are you willing to have the Universe contribute to you?

*When you ask questions you are actually co-creating with the Universe.*

We are not taught to ask questions. In school you are taught to get the answer. How much have you been programmed to get the answer, the *right* answer, and come to some sort of conclusion? In those early years, did you lose your curiosity and stop asking questions? Did your parents tell you to *stop asking so many questions!*? What would it take to crack open the door again? It takes time and practice asking questions, to eventually *live in the question.* Just start where you are. Questions are powerful tools that allow us to open up to different possibilities that we probably had not yet considered.

If you had no point of view—no answer or conclusion—what possibilities would open up when you begin to ask, "*What else is possible for me?*" "*What would I like my life to be like?*" "*What would it take to uncreate this relationship that isn't working and create something different with total ease?*" "*What beauty can be created with this breakup?*" "*If I were truly being me, what would I choose?*"

Begin to ask questions to open up some of these possibilities and expand your awareness. *What would you create if you could choose anything?* Let the question float into the Universe. Then go about you day and see what shows up.

### How much have you divorced you to stay in the relationship you are currently in? —what barriers must you break through?

Isn't it funny that in the avoidance of a breakup, you begin to divorce you instead? When you get married and "become one," what really happens to the two of you—and is there room for you? How much have you divorced you to be in your current relationship? Do you even remember who *you* are?... what you dream about?... what you'd like your future to be? We tend to lose ourselves in the entanglement of relationship, and when facing a breakup, it can feel like stepping into the great unknown—alone.

When my husband and I (as well as 3 other couples we knew) were considering divorce, it was suggested by Gary Douglas (friend, mentor and creator of these tools of consciousness) that we each take a 30-day separation to start getting clear about what we truly desired in our lives and begin moving in that direction. It was an incredible experience and if you're seriously thinking about separation, I suggest you consider it too. I know this can bring up a lot of issues: financial, time management, how to deal with the kids... however facing these issues will also occur if you decide to breakup. Why not practice using the tools, gift yourself these 30 days before you make a life changing decision? Here's how it works:

### 30 Day Experiment—moving away from routine barriers

The purpose of this experiment is to find yourself; to recognize what works for you and what you'd like to change. First, you will need to be brutally honest with yourself, willing to look at the good, and the bad—all while abstaining from judgment. If you do this, you will come away with incredible insights and new awarenesses. Some of my clients from my coaching program have even noticed that so much changed during their 30-day experiments that the relationship actually became fun again.

Each of you have a chance to take 30 days, get out of the house, out of daily routine, responsibilities, kids etc., and generate your life. Choose what you would like to do. This is not a vacation. It is an experiment to begin finding you.

Choose one of you to start, leave the house for 30 days, and go create. Maybe you would travel, or stay with friends. If you felt that in your marriage you didn't have the space or permission to do things, during this 30 days you will have the freedom to choose whatever you want. When your time is up, your partner will then leave the house and see what it is like living on their own, making their choices.

Choosing this experiment was a tremendous gift. I'm so grateful for the idea. It gave each of us the awareness of what our partner contributes to our lives, and a sense of what it would be like to live on our own. Often people think the grass is greener on the other side; couples might see the freedom that single people have and value that, while single people might value the partnership and contribution of being a couple. This experiment can give you a glimpse of another possibility.

What would you like to do, be, have, create and generate? What would it be like to live each day as an adventure? No explanation, no justification, no one to answer to... just you. Start asking questions. Find out what you really like. You might think you don't have certain choices because of your particular situation. Maybe you have kids, or don't think you can afford to live apart, or some other issue—these are all the answers or conclusions that you are perpetrating on yourself. What if you actually have choice? What else is possible? You will begin to see how living with questions open up new possibilities that did not exist before you asked.

During this 30-day journey, you will begin to recognize where you might be functioning from habitual patterns that have nothing to do with what you would choose if you were being present and including you. When you continually make choices for others, excluding yourself, where are you in the computation of your life? What would it take to start *including* you? Begin asking, "If I were being ME right now, what would I choose?"

Journal entry—written in 2010

*When we chose to do this experiment, I learned so much about our relationship—where it contributed to our life and where it did not. I got so much clarity about what I wanted to create, and how being together was actually more of a distraction. The routines we made around playing our roles according to fantasies, expectations, and judgments, hid the space where taking action and actually creating something different could be done, and where we were creating busyness to keep from creating possibilities.*

*It gave me time and distance to look at the things I was grateful for in my partner, and also acknowledge where he was not interested or capable of being/doing some of the things I desired. There were things he took care of that kept me feeling like I needed him, and with this new space I realized that I could just as easily hire someone to do those things.*

What if you begin your 30-day experiment of separation and realize that your life opens up, you're happier, and everything starts working better for you? What if it's not the same case for your spouse? This can bring up many conflicted feelings of guilt, shame, wrongness and concern for your partner. Your partner may want to resist your happiness and lightness. After all, this separation is a serious business, and how can someone be happy about it while the other is not?

You have a choice here, you can contract back down to match your partner and the energy you were being in the marriage, or you can explore this expansion and see what changes, see where it leads. What if you, choosing to be this lighter energy, changes those around you? Although you may not have a cognitive idea about what will change, being happy will create a ripple effect. What beauty could be created in your breakup? One of my clients recently reported that after her husband returned from his 30 days, the energy of their relationship had shifted so much that everything was working for both of them. They were no longer headed for divorce. She was surprised and grateful.

Choosing what feels light takes great courage and trust in your-self—trust in your awareness that choosing for you is a choice for greatness and expansion of the whole family, as well as everyone connected to you.

I wonder, if everyone on planet Earth began choosing what was light and expansive for them, what would the world look and feel like?! What beauty would be created with everyone choosing lightness? Let's just leave those questions out there to percolate in the Universe.

## Sex (or No Sex, as the case may be)

At the beginning of most intimate relationships there's typically a lot of physical touch, affection and connection. Over time it seems that as arguments, resentments and judgments come up and are not cleared (using the tools IPOV, POC & POD, and asking questions), it can create walls of separation that grow thicker and thicker, diminishing the desire to touch each other. The thicker the judgment, the greater the distance.

I remember a few months after my husband and I started dating, he told me that he was not that interested in having frequent sex. His beliefs were that it distracted from his spiritual growth. When those words came at me there was a bit of panic in my world, but I stuffed it down, walling off my own desires so I could match what he wanted. Outwardly, I focused on making the relationship work, not realizing how much of my own being I was cutting off.

Journal entry—written in 2010

*Asking for someone I would never outgrow, 23 years ago I met my husband-to-be. I knew from the moment I met him that we would get married, and actually told my mother when I got home that night, "I've met the man I'm going to marry." Awareness or decision? Good question!*

*We began dating and I can now see how I continually pushed down little awarenesses of things that didn't work for me. If I could overlook those little things, the relationship could grow. Little did I know at the time, that "relationship" means the dis-*

tance between two people, so as it grows, so does the distance. Distance between you and him, as well as between you and you.

Several months in, he mentioned that he didn't like to have that much sex, and wanted to cut back the frequency. He had a point of view that having an orgasm was taxing on his body. Wow, not great news for me! How much would I have to shut off to be ok with this? Huge amounts! And I did.

Almost a year later we moved across the country together, against my parents' wishes. My mom made me lie to my grandparents and say that I had a woman roommate. Hiding the relationship was another place where I cut off part of myself.

My dad said, "I'll give you 2 years." At the time I was in love. I thought I was fighting for the rightness of my choice. Now I realize I was being resistant and proving the rightness of my decision.

We lived together for three years before getting married. We were comfortable together, easy going companions. Sex was not a big part of our life. Occasionally I would meet other men through work and being around them I could feel the sexual energy present in their bodies. It spoke to my body as if to say, "Hey, remember this? You love this energy! It is what makes you feel alive." I would come home to my comfortable mate and all that aliveness would dissipate. I bought all that talk about how it is better to have a base in friendship, because when the sex goes, at least you like each other. Ok, cool, but do you still need to be married, or can you just be friends?

Six years later we were deeply involved with a spiritual path that advocated abstinence, or moderation sexually, which solidified the rightness of our relationship. I can see now how I choked off even more of myself, trying to be pure.

*We renewed our vows and in this organization's ceremony was the vow to bring spiritual beings to the earth and raise them consciously. A year later our daughter was born. It was a difficult birth and my husband looked like he was going to faint. He still recalls the intense event that left him stunned for years. Neither of us were interested in sex much for a while after that. Three years later we had our son. I wanted to have two kids, so they would have each other.*

*How much of my life is an invention of the fairytale trying to match the best of this reality? Meet and marry Prince Charming, have 2 beautiful children, buy a house, car, create a family-owned business... the American dream realized. Yet it feels 2 dimensional. Hollow. Missing something very important... me.*

*My entire life, I am now realizing, was an invention created to match every other person's point of view of what is good, what is important, what is significant, what is successful. No one was there to show me that something else was possible. There is a reason that having everything right in this reality is unfulfilling... you don't exist in this reality. So, perfecting it won't change the fact that you are not in the computation of your life.*

*After many sessions, clearings, body processes, I finally came to the unavoidable truth: that we were better friends than lovers. Once admitting that, much of the distance between us collapsed, and gratitude for each other emerged. Why did I wait so long to speak this? I had been using so much energy against myself to try to change it, to make our relationship work... which actually made more "work" and less fun together. Rather than trying to make something work, change it! Wouldn't you like your life to be joyful and adventurous?*

Over the years what started as a close friendship and intimate connection, grew to a distant roommate-like situation. So many couples that I have spoken to mention a similar issue in their marriages. We huddle at the edge of our side of the bed with a wall between us and our spouse. Close, but distant. Together, but apart.

Once I learned these tools, I used them religiously to try to dismantle the wall between us, yet somehow it continually grew back. I thought there was something wrong with me. I tried to convince myself that I was ok, that we were good together, and that sex didn't matter that much. The longer this went on, the more I felt worn down, older than my years, and undesirable. I sensed a push back energetically from him. But when I met other people I could feel them receiving me in a different way, a way that my husband wouldn't receive me. I longed for that affection from him.

When you are not getting your needs met physically in the relationship, it becomes quite a challenge to willingly meet your partner's. When you are married you are only supposed to receive physical affection from your spouse. What happens if you are no longer in balance sexually with each other? Do you try to turn yourself off so that you no longer want to be touched? Do you start looking outside the relationship to fulfill your desires? Do you take care of yourself? These few options seem to be what most couples choose from. What else might be possible? What if you began to talk about the issue with your partner? What if by communicating, asking questions, POC & PODing what is heavy, and using some of these tools, another possibility could surface?

When I finally summoned up the courage to speak the words out loud to my husband, "I think we're better friends than lovers," the burden that I had been carrying on my shoulders for nearly 20 years immediately dispersed. We were both in agreement. What a relief! We were both aware that things weren't working and that neither of us was actually happy. We were only trying to keep things together for the kids, for the family, for the ideals of society. None of that had anything to do with who we were, and what we wanted.

Please recognize: it takes two to create a marriage, and two to destroy it. If sex is an area where you are not finding balance, it can be a warning signal that if not addressed can cause stress, resentment, and destruction. Even if it isn't cognitive at first, our actions (namely, not being physically affectionate) spoke so loudly that we couldn't deny it any longer. The choices we made to turn off and function as roommates made it obvious to me that our marriage was nearing it's end. For couples whose sexual appetites are in balance, this may not be a problem.

---

Notes from a client interview:

*TB Spent 25 years with her husband, living mostly as platonic companions. They rarely had sex. She felt that staying in the relationship was killing her body. She tried everything from therapists, to spiritual paths, to seminars, and counselors to try to fix their relationship so it could work. Then she found the Access tools and started working with them. The Access bodywork began the process of healing her body and awakened in her the places she had shut down long ago. She realized she was living on neutral, which was actually more like dying. She decided to make a demand that her life change. She was no longer willing to kill her body in order to live in her relationship.*

---

The dissolution of our marriage was a relief for both of us, no longer having to project ourselves as the perfect couple. We rationally discussed the possibilities of what would come next. We were friends, we cared about each other, and we truly desired happiness for one another. We apologized to each other for any difficulty we caused. We dealt with every step together: selling the house, dividing up our belongings, looking at where we would be living, handling the kids etc. Nobody could believe how easy and civilized our divorce was. Even our mediator wondered if we should make a go of it and stay together. I think this is one of the benefits of having a true friendship: if/when the time comes to separate, the kindness and caring that carried you through the relationship can carry you through the breakup as well.

There need not be pain, suffering, upset, anger, ugliness, blame or regret. What would it be like if the end of your relationship was like the end of a great novel, and you could just set it down with resolve? What if by using these tools and following the energy that is most expansive for everyone involved, even dealing with children and living situations can fall into place with serendipity?

## What is best for the kids?—what "removing barriers" can open up for them

What if what is best for the kids is different than what we have decided is right? By staying together "for the kids" are we showing them how to live in contraction? Kids are aware of parents' conflict. They sense it whether or not they hear us arguing. It is an energy that is tangible. Kids sense that energy and act out.

Have you ever noticed that when you come home from a long day at work, have a lot of stress, and are upset with your spouse, your kids are often crankier too? What if that's not a coincidence?

We try to pretend that everything is ok for the benefit of the kids. What if that actually creates confusion in their world? They sense the discord, but we tell them a "non-truth" –that everything is ok–which basically invalidates their accurate awareness so they have to give up what they know in order to "trust" our lie instead. Imagine how confusing that would be to them. Is this what you really want to be teaching your children? How to *not* trust themselves, and instead trust what other people say, even though it could all be a pretense?

Have you ever met up with a friend who had just been in a big argument with their spouse and when you asked how they were, they said "Fine!" with a big smile on their face? Did you **know** that they were trying to hide the upset? Did you buy their pretense? Or did you say, "No, really,... how *are* you?" We all can sense when there has been an upset, but if we buy what people say, rather than trust our awareness, we diminish our capacity to *know what we know*. I'm not suggesting that we need to pry if someone doesn't want to talk about it; however, I am suggesting that it's not honoring of you to invalidate your awareness because someone else wants you (and him/herself) to believe the lie!

Children might have small bodies, but are very large beings! Are you acknowledging *that* in your children? Or are you thinking of them as just little kids? I have always been taken aback by the wisdom and awareness my children consistently seem to have. They have required that I acknowledge the beings that they are. I have always been determined to do my best to empower them to know what they know and to choose for themselves—even from a very early age. I remember when my daughter was just a few months old and was napping in the next room, I wanted to check on her and was too tired to get up. So in my head telepathically I asked, "Sabrina, are you ok? Let me know that you are, please?" Just then she let out a gentle sigh, and I knew that we had communicated.

All through their childhood, with both of my kids, I did things to build our ability to communicate non-verbally, telepathically. I did it because it was fun for me, and I knew that they already had the ability and I didn't want to do anything that would shut it off. Knowing that they were so aware, I was very sensitive in how I approached the subject of divorce with them.

As I'm sure you know, it is important for kids to know that divorce has nothing to do with them, that both parents love them, and that that doesn't change. I was careful to give information without any wrongness bundled in. Making your spouse wrong will most likely backfire and cause your kids to turn against you to defend the other parent. It's best to speak about what is going to occur from an objective space, rather than substantiating the breakup with reasons and wrongness on anyone's part. *Sometimes parents are not able to live happily together anymore, so there will be some changes in their living situation.*

When I was going to have a talk with my daughter, who was 11 yrs old at the time, about the fact that her dad and I were separating, she already knew that was what we were going to talk about. She said, "Oh no, are you and daddy going to get a divorce?" She had friends at school who had divorced parents and knew all about the house swapping, and awkwardness that most kids go through. I sat down with her and talked heart to heart.

That day I said to her: "You know that both daddy and I will always love and be here for you. You know that this has nothing to do with you or your brother. Do you know that you chose daddy and me as your parents, and somewhere in your universe, did you know that this would occur at some point and that you have the ability to get through it? I wonder what you know that could contribute to all of us moving through this with ease?" Right then I saw this energy of empowerment move through her; she got larger, sat up taller, became very confident... potent. She bloomed before me. She looked at me with her big eyes and said: "Mommy, everything is going to be just fine."

She had logistical questions, which I did my best to answer. "Where are we going to live? Where will we go to school? Will I be able to see both of you each week?" There was no trauma. There was no drama. There was no fear. For most people considering this choice, it's actually their own fear about what it will be like more than the child's. As you well know, our children are so aware of our thoughts and emotions, how much of the meltdown some children have when presented with the news of their parents' divorce is actually based on their perception of Mom or Dad's fears rather than their own?

Let's take a moment to talk about **fear.** Often we think we are fearful, when we are actually excited. In fact, there is no chemical difference in the body between fear and excitement—it feels the same, we just interpret the sensations based on the external context. So are you *really* afraid? Here is a way to know for sure if you even have an ounce of fear in your universe: How do you react in an emergency situation? Do you freak out and fall apart? Or do you get calm, cool and collected and handle it? If you get calm and handle things, there is no possibility of fear being in your universe (Even if you fall apart later). Unfortunately, we wait for emergency situations to realize this.

What if you were willing to claim, own and acknowledge that you have **NO fear**, and that anytime you feel those familiar pangs of panic, perhaps ask yourself, "Is this fear or excitement?" *All of the places where you have misidentified or misapplied excitement as fear, will you uncreate and destroy all of that?* POC & POD. Thank you!

By using the tools to arrive at a space of peace around our choice to get divorced, I allowed my daughter an open space to navigate from as well. There was clearly an awareness that we needed to create a new life and she wanted to be part of that creation.

My son, who was eight yrs old, really didn't seem to have a point of view about it. Again, no trauma and drama, just a willingness to move forward with a sense of wonder. Most kids wake up with this sense of wonder and joy of what is possible for that day. I'm not sure when that gets squelched out, but I can tell you, it is possible to nurture that sense of wonder back to life as an adult! What if there are no problems that need to be solved, only choices made? Who would you be each day and how would you approach living?

A client recently told me his marriage ended over a period of eight years. He and his wife decided to "play" marriage for three years living in the same house at opposite ends of the space, then for another five years living in adjacent homes. He realizes now, years later, that the choice to "keep the family together" required him to contract and diminish himself for years. Now, on the other side of divorce, he realizes that he could have been living fully and happily, while still able to be there to contribute to the kids, just not living in the same house. Hindsight...

What if you can have 20/20 vision without having to lose eight or more years of your life? With "Tool #9" (Ask: What will this choice create for my life in 5 years?) you can have clarity looking *forward*!

## Breaking out of the shell—removing barriers isn't always comfortable

Moving through a transition isn't always comfortable. Even though you may want to glue everything back in place the way it was before, take a look at it from a distance. What brought you to this moment? Things were not working for you, so you asked questions and demanded change. Here you are in this "uncomfortable" place... and yet going back is really not an option. It would be too difficult, too contractive, and if you're like anyone else who has tried to go back, you would feel like you were dying.

Trying to fit yourself back into your old relationship would be like a chick trying to go back into it's shell. At first, the cracking of the shell seems like all you want—just to get out. Then it starts breaking apart everywhere and you no longer have your warm, comfortable, small, known space to exist. There is a huge world out there with so much space, and more possibilities than you know about. But you can't glue the shell back together, and staying in the crumbling debris is not only progressively more cramped and uncomfortable, but it's not very fun either. What would it take to venture out?

It may be totally unfamiliar, and you may feel like grasping at the shell, for any point of reference to know you are ok. What if you didn't need a point of reference to know you are ok? *All of those structures, relationships and comfortable boxes that you've used* to define you as "ok", will you uncreate and destroy them, please?! POC & POD.

As you consider the possibility of leaving your relationship, your labels and reference points will change. You're no longer a wife/ husband/significant other; no longer "unavailable" for new relationships. You are freed from that box and able to choose something different. No reference points means you can create yourself as you like. What if you could be different every 10 minutes? With no one to hold you to any definition, not even yourself, wouldn't that be so exciting?! So freeing?!

And any idea that you would be scared, that you wouldn't know who you are— what if that is all bullshit? Are you really ever afraid of anything? Or have you bought that from others for so long that you believe it?! Remember: are you afraid or are you excited?! Excited about the possibilities that until now you have not been able to create?! Who would you like to be now?

As an infinite being, can you really ever know *all* that you can be, or would you be constantly expanding and changing? Locking in definitions, labels and structures is so *not* you, yet you buy that as true! Can you be in the question while removing your barriers to start getting a sense of who you would like to be?

*Everywhere you have bought all of the roles, labels and definitions of you as "who you are" will you uncreate and destroy that please?* POC & POD... What would it be like to come out of limitation and definition into infinite possibilities and continually generate from an undefined space of being? What would you create if you could choose anything?

# Step 5

## Conscious Creation

### Decadence of living

What would it be like for you if, during this time of change—which can often seem dreary and dark—you added some beauty and little bits of sunshine into your life? Just for you. After all, if you are transitioning from a relationship that isn't working to choosing what is light and will expand your life, you might as well start learning to enjoy yourself! What if it's ok to *consciously choose* to pamper yourself with a little kindness?... from YOU!

It took me a while to step into gifting kindness to myself. Usually we leave the pampering up to our partner, thinking it's selfish and self-serving to gift to ourselves. But as we talked about earlier, what if it's selfish *not* to gift to ourselves? What kindness becomes available for others when we choose for *us*?

This is one way I like to greet each day: "What can I be, do, have, create or generate today that will be more fun than I can imagine?" By asking myself this simple question, I can make every day a celebration of the joy, elegance and decadence of living... and you can too!

An essential part of *consciously creating* your new life is choosing what brings you joy. When we got divorced, we sold the house and split our belongings. I gave away all of the things that I didn't absolutely *love*, including the everyday dishes. What if *you* no longer had to hold onto old collectibles, furniture and clothing-anything that you don't absolutely adore? When you clear out those items, you are left with a sense of spaciousness and **new possibilities.**

Now I have my morning tea and toast with my grandmother's antique Sterling tea pot and my gorgeous Dior fine china set. Beautiful artwork and sparkling chandeliers adorn my home. Every time I look at them they bring me joy! I take pleasure in a clean, uncluttered home with furnishings that I love. This creates an energy that is tangible even to visitors. Although created for me and my happiness, it feels welcoming and luxurious for everyone.

What are some elements you can put into your living space that will contribute to your joy? Begin asking questions that will give you more awareness around this. *What do I desire in my home space? What would bring me joy?*

The next piece is to **honor your body** with movement and grooming. How would your body like to move? Yoga? Going for a run? Dancing? Ask your body what it would like to wear, and slip into something yummy-feeling and beautiful to see. I like to include several layers of jewelry. I enjoy choosing clothing and jewelry that feels good to my body—realizing that those choices allow me to receive their energy and contribution to my life. The more I am willing to have and acknowledge the things and people that contribute to me and my life, (as I contribute to theirs) the more I am able to increase receiving in all areas. Honoring your body helps you create the decadence of living.

Looking beautiful or handsome, taking care of your body, letting go of unwanted items, and adding some luxury to your life allows you to be more relaxed and have greater ease with receiving. More **receiving** includes energy, things and people. When you are generous with yourself you are able to contribute more to others. Whereas contracting or being stingy cuts off receiving, and often impacts our *generosity of spirit*. Having generosity of spirit is similar to having gratitude. These are generative energies that *add* to your life, and to those around you. They will assist in creating your decadent living.

Yes there are some people who may judge, "How can they be happy when they are divorcing?!" People may judge that you don't care. Are you willing to be happy in making the choice to change your relationship, rather than being unhappy stuck in it? Are you willing to receive the judgment as IPOV and not make it real, true or greater than you? Resisting or putting up barriers to judgment only makes *it* more solid and *you* at the effect. Instead, *lower your barriers* and receive the judgment–let it move through you. Imagine yourself as a **screen door** and allow the judgment to move through you like the wind.

If you are willing to be judged, and not shrink away from it, you create more receiving. After all, their judgment is just an energy that they are sending. You can use that energy to consciously create anything that you desire. If you are willing to be judged, and not make yourself wrong, (nor make the judgment right or true), eventually your strength and happiness may create curiosity and perhaps be an invitation to others to *create their lives consciously* too.

*What would you like to have as your life? What would it be like to choose what truly made you joyful? Whether anyone else agreed or not?! Will you uncreate and destroy all the imprinting and entrainment that you have been inventing yourself as, and begin to generate your conscious life?*

What would that look like? Every moment you think of it, ask questions like, What's next? Keep asking generative questions: *What would I like to do now? What would be joyful and generate a whole bunch of money? What else can I add to my life that will generate infinite future potentials?*

Just ask the questions and allow them to percolate. You don't need to have an answer. Remember, asking questions and allowing them to percolate elicits contribution from the Universe to show you new possibilities.

Embrace the possibilities of having no form, structure, or significance on anything you do. What if all of your choices were just choices, not judgeable offenses that you must constantly be looking at? How much energy are you using to analyze and judge your every move to be sure to get it right? Is it like driving your car with the emergency brake on? How much greater would your life become if instead of using all that energy to slow yourself down, you used it for constructing your amazing, phenomenal, more-fun-than-you-can-imagine life?!

## Being and Body—how to consciously create with your body

You are a Being (you may call it a soul, a higher self, etc.) that *has* a body. It is important to make a clear distinction of these. Who eats?—you or your body? Who sleeps, showers, takes walks, or has sex? These are functions of the body. Do you consider that *you are* your body and put in what *you* want rather than asking *it*? What would it be like to *ask your body* what it desires?

Many times we say, "I'm hungry," but you are the *being* and your *body* eats. So what would it be like to include your body in the computation of what concerns it? What would it take to create a connection or communion with your body?

## Tool #11: Ask your body what it desires or requires for things that concern it

What would it be like if you asked your body about things that concern it? Your body gives you clues and cues every day. Do you listen? Do you override them? When you ignore its cues, does it hurt? Would you like it to be easier? Would you like to have greater communication with your body?

One way your body lets you know things is with pictures, pains, or it may lean toward something it would like (as well as *away* from things, *and people*, it does not like). Pay attention! You will find that your body is trying to communicate with you. Listening to your body and creating an intimate connection with it will give you the ability to consciously create with your body.

If you feed your body what *it* truly desires to eat, most everything you put in your mouth will taste delicious. And when it has had enough, the flavor will decrease or change all together. Ask your body who *it* would like to sleep with and you will be surprised at how nurturing that can be. How often does your body tell you it is done, and you override it anyway, whether with food, or with people you are in relationship with? Listening to and honoring your body will dynamically improve your life experiences.

*When your body is happy, you both will feel amazing!*

What would it be like to treat your body as nicely as you do your pet? Give it love and attention, stroke it lovingly when it wakes up in the morning, ask it how it's doing. Tell it you are grateful for it. Take it out for walks, let it bask in the sun, give it plenty of water and fresh air. Imagine how it would feel if you treated it with nurturing kindness. Would it start to shine? Perk up? Feel appreciated? Look younger? Have more energy? Creating an intimate connection, or communion, with your body will help you in creating your decadence of living.

If you have difficulty in hearing what your body desires, muscle testing is an easy way to begin to make the connection. Here is a basic, easy way to begin muscle testing on yourself: Stand up straight with your feet together and hold the item in question in front of you. Let's say it is an apple. Ask, "Body, would you like to eat this?" If it pulls forward, that means "Yes"; backward means "No." Practice with whatever you like, using food, or clothing, ("Body, would you like to wear this?") until you begin to *trust your awareness*. Play with it. It will become easier the more you practice, and eventually you will just get a sense of yes or no from your body without having to stand up and ask the question.

Listening to your body will make your life more joyful. A recent client of mine was complaining of neck pain. She noticed it came on as she would go to bed at night with her husband. I asked her, "What is a pain in the neck to you?" She gasped, laughed and said, "My Husband!" When we have a point of view about a person or thing, it can register directly in our body. You might think twice before making the statement that someone is a "pain in the ass" if you don't like getting hemorrhoids!

Once we acknowledge our point of view—the pain in the neck—we can then change it. If we resist it, deny it, or any other form of avoidance, we cannot change it. So it is best to lower the barriers and look at our thoughts, creations, or points of view, and take an honest appraisal of them. Once we are willing to look at what is, we can "uncreate and destroy" all the judgments and supporting reasons and justifications—which by the way, aren't real in the first place. When you start to become clear of all those hidden POVs, you begin to function from choice, presence, being, and consciousness.

What does that look like? You ask the question, "What have I decided is a pain in the neck?" Notice if you can sense an energy come up, or possibly some words. Then you clear it all by saying, *Everything that is, I uncreate and destroy it!* POC & POD. Ask this question 5-10 times in a row and you will clear deeper levels of unconsciousness around the subject.

Holding a point of view can lock pain into our bodies. Eventually, after clearing several layers of a point of view, you will get to a place of lightness and peace. There will be no emotion attached and the pain will dissipate. Using this process is an easy way to start unlocking ourselves from these places where unconsciousness and anti-consciousness have done damage. Now you are free to consciously create your decadent living.

## Tool #12: Six months to commit to you—how to consciously create your decadent living

How do you begin living a more authentic, joyful life that is aligned with your true desires? I now realize that one of the greatest choices I made was to take a period of 6-12 months to be single, to commit to ME rather than go into relationship with someone new. Once you have moved through steps 1-4—unwinding, dissolving past trauma, gaining clarity with your own navigation, and breaking through barriers—you are freed up to begin committing to living for you. It may feel different, uncomfortable, and you might feel like you could slip back into giving it all up for your next relationship. So, what if instead, you chose to **commit to you** rather than doing relationship for at least 6 - 12 months? This may be a really big challenge. It was difficult for me at first. But the result was so worth it.

What does committing to your living look like? I still went out and met people. But rather than head-tripping over thoughts about what it could be like to spend my future with each new man, I enjoyed one date... and learned a lot about myself. I learned what my priorities were, what I really desired, and what it was like to have my own back.

What is committing to you? No relationship for *six months*? What?! No sex?! Yes, you can have sex, but only once with a person, and no sleep-overs. What happens when you have sex more than once with someone? Most people automatically go into relationship, focus on the other person and give *themselves* up. Have a look at it for yourself and you will likely realize the truth of this. Only having one date keeps you in the present. This was recommended to me after my divorce to have more of a sense of who I am and what I would like. I had spent so much of my life in relationship that I had no idea of who I was, or what I really wanted.

At first this commitment was difficult because of the habitual tendency of projecting out into the future—even on the first date! I didn't realize that I did that to such an extreme. How about you? Do you meet someone, maybe for drinks, and start to wonder what it would be like to move in together? What would it be like to just be present and stay in the moment? Can you enjoy their company without those projections?

Committing to my life also strengthened my ability to perceive which direction the attraction was coming from. Was I truly attracted to them or were they attracted to me? Many times on a first date thought I was attracted to the person sitting across from me. Then I'd go home and have a totally different awareness. I'd ask myself; "Am I attracted to them or are they attracted to me?" Asking the question gave me the awareness of what was true for me.

The consecutive months of committing to my life gave me so much more awareness of where and when I would cut off what I wanted for the other person's desires. I realized that it was so much easier to know what they wanted than what I wanted. I would divorce myself for their happiness. Do you have the same point of view? When the focus is on trying to make others happy, there is a tendency to lose awareness of your own happiness. What would it take to have awareness of their desires, as well as your own, and choose from that space? Committing to your life builds your trust in yourself. Imagine what it would be like to have your own back, and choose what would work for you, instead of squashing you to have something work for them?

I also got clear that there is a choice point where we can go either way—expand or contract—and that I was making a demand of myself to follow the lightness of expansion. This is committing to your living. It is not necessarily logical or rational. Ask questions, follow the lightness, and maintain awareness of what works for you. When you commit to you, and trust yourself, your life will expand.

Start to get some clarity on what it is that you would like. Spend some time with yourself, look at the elements that you would like to have in a relationship. Take time to also look at the things that don't work for you and start to get a sense of what it would actually be like to be with somebody that is a contribution to your life. A contributory relationship is where the person does not become your life, but adds to your life, and you add to theirs.

## The Truth About Passion

Do you believe that passionate romances are the pinnacle of all relationships? A lot of books talk about following your passion. I'm suggesting something different–follow your lightness. Think back on all of your passionate relationships—how did they turn out? Was it everything you hoped it would be? Or was it a lot more difficult than you would have liked? Well, have I got some interesting information for you!

If you look up the definition of passion in an old dictionary (printed prior to 1946, when definitions became altered) you will find it says something like this: *Passion = to suffer; the fact or state of enduring inflicted pain, tortures, or the like.*

So when you ask for a passionate relationship, or to follow your passion, are you really sure that's your best choice?! What about asking for nurturing, contributory relationships? I know, I know, most people hear that and think, "Boring!" So *what have you misidentified and misapplied nurturing as that doesn't allow you to have fun and contribution in your relationships? Will you let all of that go and see what else can show up?!* POC & POD. I wonder what else is possible with fun, playful, nurturing and contributory partners?!

Let's do an exercise that will hopefully create some space and freedom for you around past (or present) relationships where there is that energy of passion that might be torturing you. Get the person in mind and the energy of what being in relationship with them is for you. Intensify it—more, more, and even more! Ok, feel that? Now I'd like to ask you, how many times have you killed each other in other lifetimes? You may notice a lot of energy come up, sense a tightening in places of your body (and you may not sense anything, and that's ok too). *Everything that brought up, will you uncreate and destroy it?* (This allows the energy to shift and flow where before it was locked up and stuck. Your willingness is all that is required for it to shift) POC & POD... Breathe...

This might sound weird, but, *Whose turn is it to kill whom in this lifetime? Everything that is, will you uncreate and destroy it?* POC & POD. (Repeat these questions followed by the clearing POC & POD several times until there is no energy on the person for you).

Now, think of the person, the relationship you had—do you feel any different about them/it now? Once we have cleared all of the unconscious, stuck energy we have with passion, our perception of the relationship will most likely feel different. Most of the time people report that what was a compelling, almost out-of-control drive, calms to a sense of neutrality. You can have it or not have it. This is the space of true choice.

## Moving into Action—getting out of reaction into conscious action

How much are you in reaction to everything and everyone in your life?! Reaction can take the positive side of agreement, or the negative side of resistance. Are you creating your life in agreement or alignment with what other people do, say, impose, or think is right for you? Do you find you are also in resistance to their shoulds, shouldn'ts and subjective points of view?

Most of my life, I was in *resistance* to what other people said or thought. Even though I had an awareness that it wasn't my best choice, my resistance kept me locked in. Wherever you are in resistance and reaction, or alignment and agreement, you are not able to create anything different for yourself!

This reality is all about how things are unchangeable, immutable, and that's all there is to it. But does that feel light to you? Or heavy? Remember, if it's light it's true, if it's heavy it's a lie. So how many lies are we buying, believing things are immutable in this reality? Tons!

Growing up I had the usual pressures to conform, from family, peers, teachers and society, as I'm sure you did as well. A while back I got a huge eye-opening awareness with this tool of moving into action. One of the decisions I made as a young woman was still running me decades later because I was in *resistance* to what everyone was telling me to do. (Don't you just love to do what you're *not* supposed to do, or conversely, *not* do what you're supposed to?!) Funny creatures we are that we love to try to overcome the *not*. Unfortunately we don't always look at what that will create. We're too busy proving someone wrong. What if we didn't have to resist and react in order to choose? What if we could create more, easier, faster, and with more fun? How, you ask? By moving beyond this old program!

I remember the moment I told my grandmother about a man I met that I was beginning to date. She asked if he shared our same religious background, and when I said no, she ordered me to "get rid of him!" I was in such resistance to her insistence, that I ended up marrying him and stayed married for 20 years. Unconsciously I was proving how right I was, and how wrong she was, even though underneath I wasn't happy with my decision. (I say "decision" here because I had turned my choice into an unchangeable solidity by being in reaction to her.)

The relationship and our life together wasn't all bad. That's not what I'm saying. It was the resistance, the overriding, the no-choice-but-to-prove-her-wrong point of view, that stuck me. I was in reaction, not action. Your situation may be completely different, but can you look for the places you are in reaction that keep you locked up? Now, how do you move out of this place of reaction and choose something different?

**Taking action** allows you to access something different. It can be as simple as asking a question, *What action can I take that will change this?* When you ask a question and allow the universe to provide responses, without having a point of view what it needs to look like, amazing possibilities present themselves. You will see everything that seemed solid and unchangeable melt before you. This is what is called creating your own reality... your decadent living. When you buy into the immutable laws of this reality, you create the destruction of you, your life and your possibilities. Which would be more fun for you? Are you willing to try asking questions, shift into taking action, and watch this reality change?

*If I choose this, what will it create for my future? What other possibilities are there that I have not yet considered? What action can I take today to create my decadent living? What do I truly desire?*

Questions create awareness. Questions create possibilities. Questions allow the universe to show you something different.

Just for today, see what it would be like to live in the question. What would it be like to be the leader of your decadent life? Who am I today, and what grand and glorious adventures await me?® What would I like to do next? What else is possible?

# Step 6

## Maintenance System

### Peace of mind & confidence

What would it be like to continue to trust you and build confidence? As you start asking questions, sensing what is light and true for you, and choosing lightness, you begin to be more congruent with yourself. Gather momentum. Try not to second guess yourself. Just choose, and if it doesn't turn out the way you like, choose again. Build strength with continued practice, and move forward with a sense of peace and true confidence. Know that you create your future and that you have choice.

*During this process, will you please allow time to practice and strengthen your commitment to you? Everything that doesn't allow that, will you uncreate and destroy it? POC & POD.*

What would it take to have allowance for yourself, and back off any self-judgement that may arise during this process? What if you were to treat yourself at least with as much kindness and caring as you do your child, your friends, or your pet? Do you give them the attention, nurturing, and loving that they need to grow healthy and strong? Why wouldn't you do that for yourself as well?

Every judgment that you have of yourself stops anything you have been creating. Who knows better how to stop you and hurt you than you? What do you do that for? And are you willing to stop judging yourself now? Judgment stops you from choosing or creating. Judgment is toxic, ugly, and kills your body.

NEWS FLASH: Judgment is *not real*, it is a *creation*. That means that we create it, or buy it from others, and are making it real and greater than us. What else might be possible if you were to POC & POD judgment, and instead have kindness and caring for you?

Years ago, after using these tools to expand my awareness, I had a realization about judgment. I used to think people were judging me, as well as others, and would I shrink back or change my behavior as a result. As I was looking back over my life, I realized that I never really judged anyone else, just myself. Then I had the awareness that perhaps that's what most people are doing as well!

What if the person who you think is judging you about your "failing relationship," for example, is actually judging him/herself about his/her own crappy relationship?! What if your willingness to change what isn't working in your marriage brings up the harsh reality that they are not happy and don't yet have the courage to step into taking action to change it? When we feel judged, what if it really is just *them judging themselves*?

*Everything is the opposite of what it appears to be, and nothing is the opposite of what it appears to be. Breathe...*

One of my clients mentioned that after his divorce he always felt judged by his neighbors. He thought they were judging him for divorcing. He would shrink energetically around them. When I asked him, "Is that yours, someone else's, or something else?" he realized that it wasn't his! He came to the awareness that it was actually the neighbors who were jealous of his new freedom.

It doesn't really matter where judgment comes from, the key is to realize that it's not yours, nor real, and then come out of being at the effect of it. If that makes you feels lighter, consider the possibility that it is true. And this brings us to our final tool in this book: Choice.

## Tool #13: Choice!

*What if you don't have to figure out how to clear something?!*

So many times you hear people trying to figure out the way out of the mess they are in. Has that ever worked? If you could figure it out, would you be in the mess in the first place? And yet we continue to do the same thing! We're cute, but not very bright! With these tools, it is possible to clear out all those old habits and unconscious thoughts that keep us moving in circles. We say the clearing statement, POC & POD, and then we are free from those limitations.... But you still need to *choose* what's next!

Choice actually creates change in your life faster than processing or clearing out all of your limitations. You don't need to work that hard. Just choose. And if you get stuck, then you can use a clearing tool from this book to get you moving again.

*Make a different choice and see what shows up!*

If you find that you run the clearings on yourself all the time, but nothing is changing, chances are good that you are still choosing the same things while expecting a different result. If you keep running into the same experiences in your future that you were trying to get away from in the past, what might be missing is making a different *conscious choice*.

How do you make a conscious choice? You choose from your awareness. Most people are trying to make the RIGHT choice instead of just choosing and finding out what is LIGHT. You have to do all kinds of judgment before you make a choice to see which choice is going to be *right*. Remember, choosing from awareness of what's *light* is a completely different way of functioning. As you play with each of these tools, you will continue to build your awareness.

Now, building the muscle of awareness can take time. Be patient with yourself. And please, be kind! Just like going to the gym to build physical muscle, working out several times a week will be more effective than once in awhile. And sometimes you will require some help, a trainer or a coach, to help you incorporate your new healthy practice. So as you build your muscle of awareness, you may benefit from the assistance of a coach or facilitator. Reach out to me if you'd like some help with building your awareness and creating beauty in your transition.

When looking at our own choices it is not always easy to be objective and *not* be vested in a particular outcome. Have you ever noticed how it is easier to be objective for other people rather than yourself? If you are vested, you already have an answer in place, and therefore are not in your awareness. At those choice points, if I am feeling confused or can't get clarity around the energy by using these tools, I'll call a friend or schedule a session with a facilitator.

Let's say I have three choices that I'm considering and would like assistance getting clear on my awareness. I'll call a friend and tell her the choices, ask her to mix up the order and have her ask me, "Which one will create the future you'd like to have, A, B or C?" That way I can sense the energy of each choice without being biased by my point of view about what it is. If you have a friend that can be totally objective, this can work really well.

Another option is to find a coach or **facilitator**. A facilitator will empower you to know what you know. We are trained to provide a space for you to have your awareness more substantially than on your own. We have also built our muscle of awareness that will assist in pointing you to the precise places where you might be sticking yourself, and provide the space for you to make the changes you desire. It is great for beginning your training of building strength and confidence in your own knowing. I highly recommend you find a facilitator that you can work with, at least to get you started.

## The Value of Acknowledgment—
## how to build trust and confidence

What else does it take to build and maintain the muscles of awareness that will lead you to your decadent living? Acknowledgement. Do you acknowledge that you know? Or do you doubt yourself, your choices, or your ability to do or choose something? When building the muscles of awareness, doubt and invalidation take you back several steps. Your awareness muscles actually weaken.

Begin looking at the things you've been asking for. Do you have the point of view that you don't have them yet? Is *something* showing up, no matter how small? Is there *any* difference? If the answer is yes, you may be invalidating what you have created by only looking for the end result instead of acknowledging the incremental change. When we doubt and invalidate ourselves along the way, it's like taking the nails back out of the house we're building. You may get there eventually, but you're undoing the change and adding to the work.

How many times have you asked for more affection from your spouse, for example, and never acknowledged the incremental increases because they were "not enough." That invalidation of "not enough" is a judgment. Judgment stops the energy. So if you would like to keep the flow of affection between you increasing, just keep asking, "Cool that this is starting to show up! How does it get *any better* than this?"®

*Anywhere you have come to the conclusion or judgment that things are not changing, rather than acknowledging what has changed, and continuing to ask for more, will you uncreate and destroy all of that please?* POC & POD.

## There is power in acknowledging

Acknowledgment allows you to see what *is* from a place of non-judgment. It allows you to build on the changes that you are creating. Every acknowledgment allows you to take another giant step forward with confidence that you are going in the direction you desire to go. Every invalidation, or judgment that it isn't working or changing, takes you several steps backward or stops you completely.

## What does acknowledgment look like?

How can you acknowledge yourself? You say (or think to yourself), *I created that!* or *How cool that more is showing up?! Wow, the universe really does have my back.*

It is just for you, just for fun, you don't have to tell anyone. You don't need to tell your partner, your friends, your work associates, or the world. Just know that you know, and smile.

---

Here's a story to give you an example:

*A girlfriend wanted to go out dancing and have flirty fun with her husband and their friends. They went to check out a band and it wasn't quite what they were looking for. After a few drinks, she suggested to head back to their house and do some karaoke on their tv. The guys sat on the couch with drinks and watched the girls sing and laugh and have a great time. After their friends left, rather than watching a movie and going to bed, her husband put on some of his favorite music and they danced in the kitchen. He gazed deeply into her eyes as they danced. She longed for this connection, had asked for it, and here it was showing up in their kitchen. She was grateful. She had asked, and although it showed up different than what she had imagined, she enjoyed the playful, flirty fun that came from her request. Silently she acknowledged and wondered, "Cool, how does it get any better?"*

---

So, acknowledging what is showing up, rather than judging what isn't, will build momentum. The more you acknowledge you, what you know, who you be, and what is possible, the quicker you will find your dreams materializing all around you!

## The value of caring—having gratitude for what you have actually contributes to your peace of mind

Do you take care of your things, keep them clean, and well maintained? Ever notice that your favorite jeans, or suit, or even your car can look like new even if they are "old"? When we give the energy of caring, appreciation and gratitude to our possessions (as well as our partner) they respond by looking just like new! This doesn't take effort, just a willingness on your part. It is a generative energy that feels good to BE and use. Have a look through your life and see if you can find at least one example. Now think about how you appreciate it being in your life.

Go ahead, I'll wait... .

Ok, got it? So, truth, did that item or person *gift to you* as you appreciated it? Yes?! Isn't that cool?

What you appreciate, and have **gratitude** for, actually contributes *to you* as well! It expands your life!! And conversely, if you withhold that energy, things tend to age and fall apart sooner. It's like that multidimensional generosity of spirit I was talking about earlier.

Having gratitude for your partner as well as yourself may be a new concept. Were you taught to criticize, undermine, and invalidate each other? As if criticizing makes you want to do better! What would it be like to have gratitude instead? Even in separation there can be gratitude.

Notes from client interview:

*RB realizes that he has not been a good husband, that he has never really been there for his wife, or for himself. He went on his 30-day journey to find his life and uncovered huge areas where he was shut down. He is now willing to look at his life and behavior from his wife's point of view, and has so much gratitude for her. He realizes he was acting like an asshole. And he didn't blame her for wanting to leave.*

So go forth, and know that there is nothing to fear. Fear is not real. Make those changes that seem insurmountable by asking for what you really want, whether it's breaking up, or simply making changes to your relationship so it works for both of you. You don't have to know *how* it will show up, that's the Universe's job.

Realize for yourself, that you can have the life of your dreams if you are willing to have the courage to ask for and choose it, continually along the way. Trust yourself. Be kind to you. Choose what is light. Have fun! Be happy! Isn't that what you wanted in your relationship in the first place?

If you are willing to work with these steps, you are on your way to consciously creating a beautiful life and living. Who are you today, and what grand and glorious adventures will you have? If you have come to the place where your next step includes breaking up, what beauty can you create along the way?

# Appendix A

## Steps Recap

**Steps 1-2** Bars, Interesting Point of View, and asking, "What else is possible?" all work together to create space.

**Steps 3-4** assist you in navigating what is LIGHT and true for you, making different choices for your future.

**Steps 5-6** are about adding you into the computation, having the decadence, peace and confidence to create beauty and joyful aliveness in your life.

# Appendix B

# Tools Recap

**Tool #1: Lower your barriers, and go into question: "What is true for me?"**

Only when you're willing to be honest with yourself and look at what is true for you, can you begin to change things. Lower your barriers and be vulnerable with yourself. True vulnerability is not having any barriers to your awareness. Ask questions from curiosity. Simply ask and then let them percolate; allow the questions to go out into the universe and notice when responses show up.

**Tool #2: To begin to get free of your own decisions and conclusions, start seeing everything as an Interesting Point of View (IPOV)**

"Interesting point of view I have this point of view. Interesting point of view they have that point of view." Using this tool moves you into being in allowance. When you are in allowance, you are no longer at the effect of other people's IPOVs.

**Tool #3: The Bars**

This energetic body treatment clears the mind and creates space and peace in your body. It is a great way to erase the stress and fear that often comes up around breakups. Any time you feel overwhelmed, stressed, confused, tired, etc. get your Bars run. You will feel like a new person with more space for possibilities.

**Tool #4: Uncreate all your Points of Creation & Points of Destruction (POC & POD) to erase the past**

This tool is like a magic wand that releases the energetic ties to old beliefs, judgments and decisions. It creates clarity and expands your ability to choose what will work for you. We call using this tool "running a process." We run the process and POC & POD until the energy changes, and often physical limitations disappear too.

**Tool #5: Where there is gratitude, there is no room for judgment**

Practice having gratitude for things in your life. Gratitude is a generative energy and will create more of what you are grateful for.

**Tool #6: If it's Light, it is true; If its Heavy, its a lie**

Choosing possibilities that are light and expansive will create more joy and ease. Choosing what is heavy will most likely lead to difficulty and unhappiness. This is your energetic awareness of what those choices will create in your future. Pay attention to it and practice.

**Tool #7: Ask, "Is this mine, someone else's, or something else?" and return it all to sender**

This tool begins to show you how many of the thoughts/feelings/emotions you have bought as your own that do not originate from you and requires you to acknowledge of how psychic you are. Most of the time just asking lightens up the awareness. You will have more peace of mind if you practice this for 3 days.

**Tool #8: Everything is the opposite of what it appears to be, and nothing is the opposite of what it appears to be**

Repeat this phrase to get out of your mind's circular thinking when you can't seem to stop. May need to repeat 3-10 times.

**Tool #9: Ask, "If I make this choice, what would my life be like in 5 years?"**

Immediately after you ask the question, an energy will come up. Notice what it feels like in your body. Just sense it and let it go, and then look at the other side, "If I don't choose this, what will my life be like in 5 years?" Consider asking for then another choice, and another, to sense into which direction to navigate to toward the future you'd like to create.

**Tool #10: Live in the Question**

Ask questions, they open up possibilities. Answers close the door. Allow the questions to be. Don't try to get the answer. Don't try to figure anything out. Just ask, and let them to go out into the Universe and create possibilities for you.

**Tool #11: Ask your body what it desires or requires for things that concern it**

You are a Being that has a Body. Your body gives you cues every day. Ask it questions about things that concern it, and pay attention. When your body is happy, you both will be happy.

**Tool #12: 6 Months to commit to you—how to consciously create your decadent living**

Chose to **commit to you** rather than doing relationship for at least 6 - 12 months. This will give you time to build your awareness of what you would like, rather than falling into the habitual pattern of giving yourself up for a relationship.

**Tool #13: Choice!**

Choice actually creates change faster than processing or clearing out all of your limitations. You don't need to work that hard. Just choose. And if you get stuck, then you can use a clearing tool from this book to get you moving again.

# Appendix C
## Unwinding Audio

Listening to this audio will create space, relaxation, and help you unwind. You can even "loop" it on very low volume while you sleep to create deeper clearing.

**www.julietutonenergy.com/possibilities**

# About the Author

Coming from Boston, Julie Tuton has an East Coast edge, softened by over 25 years of living in the San Francisco Bay Area. She has a razor sharp awareness that allows her to cut through to the core of your issues with kindness and caring.

She lives in the space of non-judgment, allowing her to be very real and present with you. Applying her awareness and practical tools to step into places of change in her own personal life, she comes from a place of vulnerability, compassion, and knowing that if she could move through such transitions with ease, she can facilitate others to do so as well.

*Going through a breakup or divorce is difficult. I've been there and I understand your struggle. I also know something else is possible. In ending a 20 year marriage, I used these tools to facilitate my transition. So many people commented and inquired about the ease of our separation and divorce, wondering what I had done that was so different. Even our mediator was curious. I wrote* Beauty in the BreakUp *for everyone who is seeking a different possibility navigating this often treacherous area of change.*

*What if you could create your breakup with kindness for everyone involved, and move forward in lightness and beauty?*

*– Julie*

If you would like to follow up with more in depth study of these tools and processes, are curious about coaching, classes, or have interest in private sessions with Julie, her contact information is below:

**www.beautyinthebreakup.com**

**www.julietutonenergy.com**

**julietutonenergy@gmail.com**

CPSIA information can be obtained
at www.ICGtesting.com
Printed in the USA
FSOW03n2320240118
43689FS